LETTERS ★ FROM ★ THE ★ HOMEFRONT

WORLD WAR I

LINDA S. GEORGE

BENCHMARK BOOKS

MARSHALL CAVENDISH
NEW YORK

Benchmark Books
Marshall Cavendish Corporation
99 White Plains Road
Tarrytown, New York 10591-9001
Website: www.marshallcavendish.com

Library of Congress Cataloging-in-Publication Data
George, Linda S., 1949–
World War I / by Linda S. George.
Includes bibliographical references and index.
Summary: Describes the impact of World War I on life in the United States, discussing such topics as propaganda, prejudices against immigrants and African-Americans, opposition to the war, and women's roles.
ISBN 0-7614-1096-1 (lib. bdg.)
1. World War, 1914–1918—United States—Juvenile literature. 2. Soldiers—United States—Correspondence—Juvenile literature. 3. World War, 1914–1918—Personal narratives, American—Juvenile literature. [1. World War, 1914–1918—United States. 2. World War, 1914–1918—Personal narratives, American.] I. Title: World War One. II. Title. III. Series.
D640.A2 G47   2001   940.4'8173—dc21   00-036027

Book design by Carol Matsuyama
Photo research by Anne Burns Images
Printed in Italy   .
6 5 4 3 2 1

Photo Credits

Cover Photo by: Bridgeman Art Library
The photographs in this book are used by permission and through the courtesy of: *Archive Photos*: 8, 47, 53, Hulton Getty. *Corbis*: Bettman 2, 16, 17, 21, 28, 31, 35, 41, 49, 50, 51, 67, 76. *SuperStock*: 13, David Spindel, 30, 72. Stock Montage, 43. *Library of Congress*: 23, 55, 71, 84. *Liaison*: Hulton Getty, 52, 63, 74. *Art Resource*: 80.

ACKNOWLEDGMENTS

With thanks to Glenn C. Altschuler, the Thomas and Dorothy Litwin Professor of American Studies, Cornell University, Ithaca, New York, for his expert reading of the manuscript.

Special thanks to Virginia Schomp, who developed the concept for the LETTERS FROM THE HOMEFRONT series.

Grateful acknowledgments are made to the following individuals, organizations, and publishers for permission to reprint these materials:

Joseph Gaffney correspondence, January 18, 1918; February 8, 1918; March 14, 1918; April 30, 1918; May 19, 1918; November 11, 1918; Gaffney-Ahearn Family Correspondence, Manuscripts and Archives Division, The New York Public Library, Astor, Lenox and Tilden Foundations.

Minnie Parkhurst and Sarah Cohen to A. Mitchell Palmer, April 12, 1919; and Louise Olivereau to Minnie Parkhurst, March 22, 1920; Louise Olivereau Letters, Manuscripts and Archives Division, The New York Public Library, Astor, Lenox and Tilden Foundations.

Leopold Stokowski to Woodrow Wilson, August 20, 1918; Woodrow Wilson Papers, series 4, file 4444, Library of Congress.

"Address to the Committee on Public Information," June 1918, from *A Documentary History of the Negro People in the United States: From the Emergence of the N.A.A.C.P. to the Beginning of the New Deal, 1910–1932,* edited by Herbert Aptheker, Citadel Press, 1973.

Letters to the *Chicago Defender*, October 17, 1916; March 11, 1917; April 21, 1917; April 30, 1917; May 5, 1917; May 11, 1917; May 19, 1917; from "Letters of Negro Migrants of 1916-1918" published in the *Journal of Negro History*, July 1919, October 1919.

Excerpts from "Central High" and excerpt from "I've Known Rivers" from The Big Sea by Langston Hughes. Copyright © 1940 by Langston Hughes. Copyright renewed © 1968 by Arna Bontemps and George Houston Bass. Reprinted by permission of Hill and Wang, a division of Farrar, Straus and Giroux, LLC.

Mrs. W. S. to the Children's Bureau, January 30, 1918; from *Raising a Baby the Government Way: Mothers' Letters to the Children's Bureau, 1915–1932,* by Molly Ladd-Taylor, Rutgers University Press, 1986.

Martha L. Wilchinski to Bill, [nd]; from *"Dear Folks at Home": The Glorious Story of the United States Marines in France As Told by Their Letters from the Battlefield,* edited by Kemper Frey Cowing, Houghton Mifflin, 1919.

"Our Service Flag," poem by Langston Hughes, from *Central High Monthly*, March 1918, in the Western Reserve Historical Society, Cleveland, Ohio.

To the memory of
Charles J. Poole,
a soldier in the Great War

CONTENTS

FROM THE AUTHOR

In some ways, I have wanted to write this book since I was a little girl. I grew up in Cleveland, Ohio, but my family came from a small town in North Carolina, and every summer we visited my grandparents and other relatives there. My grandfather was quiet and gentle, but he also seemed a little mysterious to me. My mother had told me that he had lost his hearing in World War I. He was shell-shocked, she said. I was not quite sure what that meant. I knew it had something to do with bombs and gunfire going off nearby, and later I learned about the trenches in France, where my grandfather had fought. I remember a photo of my grandfather as a young man, his hair still black, standing with his war buddies on a little street in France, smiling. When we visited my grandparents in the summer, everyone laughed and told funny stories. No one wanted to talk about a horrible, far-off war that happened long ago. I never asked my grandfather about the war. He died when I was twelve.

Often people don't want to remember wars, and particularly they don't like to remember wars like World War I. Historians have said that the war should not have happened, that diplomats should have been able to negotiate peace before war exploded and so quickly became so horrendous. Americans would like to forget some of what went on in the United States during the war, too. People who lived through the First World War did not come to be known as the Greatest Generation, as journalist Tom Brokaw has termed those who lived through World War II. Instead, they were called the Lost Generation, people who came out of a senseless, brutal war disillusioned and broken.

The books in this series, LETTERS FROM THE HOMEFRONT, tell the story of the United States' major wars not through the battles and

WITH LOVE to all my DEAR ONES.

It's ages since I saw you
now it seems,
But your presence
ever in my memory
gleams,-
Here's my
love to all at
home,-
Till I'm back no more
to roam
I shall always have
you with me in
my dreams.
Roses for Love.-
White Heather for Luck.

IN TIMES OF WAR, LETTERS ARE THE SOLDIER'S LIFELINE.

pronouncements of kings and presidents, but through the words of people at home. People on the homefront recorded their thoughts in diaries, they wrote letters to soldiers and friends, and they spoke about the war. Their words can help us understand these important events in American history as those who lived them understood them.

My family has moved many times and we have lost track of the letters and other souvenirs our relatives might have kept. I suppose that may be part of the reason I was particularly drawn to a collection of letters I found in the New York Public Library. Private Joseph Gaffney was a young man from New York City who volunteered for service in the army. He had five sisters, and they and his parents, cousins, aunts, uncles, and friends all wrote letters to Joe, and he wrote back. These letters—hundreds of them— were given by the family to the library and are now kept in several boxes in the Rare Books and Manuscripts Collection.

I spent many, many hours reading through these letters. I

came to recognize sister Florrie's looped, graceful handwriting and her pink stationery, and Joe's father's elegant scrawl. Sometimes the letters made me cry, sometimes I laughed, but I always felt a wonderful, warm glow, as if I were part of this family, as if I were living the war with them, hopeful and determined. I also felt very grateful that the Gaffneys had put the letters in a place where they will not get lost, where others can read them. I have included several letters from the Gaffney family in this book. They are full of fascinating details of what was happening "on the homefront" during the war. They are also a poignant reminder of the human side of war, of the fears just beneath the surface, the feelings of powerlessness, the resolve to present a cheerful face, no matter what.

The Gaffney letters and the other letters, diaries, and memoirs included in this book tell the story from the homefront during World War I. These pieces were written by people who did not know how the story was going to end. They did not know if their loved ones were going to come back from the war, they did not know the shape the world would take once the war was over, and they did not know how very different life at home would be after the war.

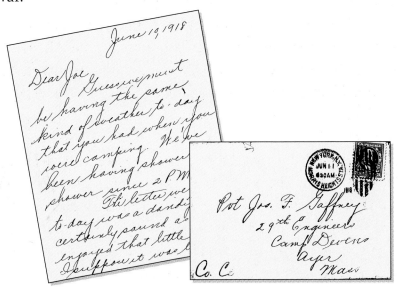

INTRODUCTION: THE GREAT WAR

On June 28, 1914, in Sarajevo, the capital of Bosnia in southern Europe, an assassin leaped into the open car of Archduke Franz Ferdinand of Austria and killed the nobleman and his wife. This event lit the fuse that exploded into the Great War, or World War I.

Archduke Franz Ferdinand was heir to the throne of Austria-Hungary and commander of the Austrian army. His country had recently made Bosnia part of Austria-Hungary, and many Bosnians were outraged. Bosnian nationalists had plotted with military officers from Serbia, a neighboring country, to assassinate the archduke, in the hope of winning independence. Serbia's involvement in the assassination was discovered, and Austria-Hungary came down harshly on Serbia. Serbia refused to accept Austrian demands, and on July 28, 1914, Austria-Hungary declared war on Serbia.

It quickly became clear that this was not going to remain a little war confined to a small country in southern Europe. All the nations of Europe had been expecting war. For many years rival countries had been making treaties and alliances, and by 1914 Europe was divided into two camps. Germany and Austria-Hungary were members of the Triple Alliance, or Central Powers. Russia, France, and England formed the rival Triple Entente Powers (later they were called the Allies). The archduke's assassination only sparked a fire that was long heating up. After Austria-Hungary declared war on Serbia, Russia immediately began mobilizing troops to defend Serbia. In response, Austria-Hungary and its ally Germany declared war on Russia. France stepped in to defend Russia, declaring war on Germany. Great Britain, France's ally, declared war on Germany, too.

Germany had long been ready for war and had a plan to attack France, its neighbor to the west, first, and then Russia, in the east. In the early days of August 1914, Germany blasted through Belgium and Luxembourg and tore into France, where most of the war would be fought.

Americans watched in horror as the events in Europe unfolded. A *New York Times* editorial condemned the conflict: "The European nations have reverted to the condition of savage tribes roaming in the forest and falling upon each other in a fury of carnage." Another newspaper editor wrote, "We have never appreciated so keenly as now the foresight exercised by our forefathers in emigrating from Europe."

The United States tried to stay out of the conflict. Most Americans wanted nothing to do with foreign wars. Isolationism—keeping out of what Thomas Jefferson had termed "entangling alliances"—was deeply ingrained in American politics. Americans in 1914 were particularly determined to keep a distance from Europe's problems. But despite their resolve, they were drawn in as German submarines sank American ships, along with those of other nations, and killed American passengers. On U.S. soil, Americans discovered German and Austrian spies committing acts of sabotage. As Americans grew more and more alarmed, Britain, using a barrage of propaganda, worked hard to persuade the United States to join its cause.

In April 1917—nearly three years after the fighting began—the United States entered the war. In June General John J. Pershing, commander of U.S. forces in Europe, arrived in France with a handful of soldiers. Over the next months, more than two million American recruits—fresh, strong, and enthusiastic but poorly trained—poured into France. The U.S. reinforcements helped turn the tide. Germany and its allies were defeated, and peace was declared on November 11, 1918.

The Great War had involved most of Europe as well as countries in Asia, Africa, and North and South America. In all, some 65 million people fought in the war and, in little more than four years, about 9 million lost their lives. It was a senseless, savage war that sent wave after wave of young men to be cut down by automatic guns or blown to pieces by land mines. Much of the war was fought in muddy, stinking trenches, where men battled lice and rats, disease and despair, as well as the enemy. The war kindled hatreds that would smolder and burst into an even mightier flame twenty years later in the Second World War.

The World War—as it was sometimes called then, since no one yet imagined there could be a second one—forced Americans to rethink much of what they had taken for granted. They had to consider how they felt about the United States as a haven for immigrants. They had to think about democracy and just how free people ought to be to speak their minds. They were faced with either accepting or challenging racism. And they had to consider just what was meant by a "woman's place" in American society.

IN APRIL 1917 NEWSPAPERS ACROSS THE COUNTRY
BLAZED WITH HEADLINES THAT THE UNITED STATES HAD
ENTERED THE WAR.

Countries at War

Central Powers	Major Allied Powers
Germany, Austria-Hungary, The Ottoman Empire (Turkey), Bulgaria	The British Empire, France, Russia, the United States

1

MAKING THE WORLD "SAFE FOR DEMOCRACY"

Over there, over there,
Send the word, send the word, over there
That the Yanks are coming, the Yanks are coming
. . . .
We'll be over, we're coming over,
And we won't be back till it's over over there.

—"OVER THERE,"
COMPOSED BY GEORGE M. COHAN
ON THE DAY THE U.S. DECLARED WAR ON GERMANY

Going to War

On April 2, 1917, President Woodrow Wilson asked the U.S. Congress to declare war on Germany. "We will not choose the path of submission!" the president declared. The United States would fight "for the ultimate peace of the world and for the liberation of its peoples. . . . The world must be made safe for democracy."

The United States had come a long way since August 1914,

when President Wilson had urged Americans not to take sides. "The United States must be neutral in fact as well as in name during these days that are to try men's souls," he had said. "We must be impartial in thought as well as in action."

President Wilson had hoped to keep the United States out of Europe's war, and most Americans wanted to stay out. But a series of events pushed Americans into the conflict. One of the major factors was German submarine warfare. Early in the war, the British navy had blockaded Germany, keeping neutral countries—the United States among them—from shipping goods, including food, to the Central Powers. The Germans retaliated with their submarines, threatening not only the military ships of the Allies but also civilian vessels.

On May 7, 1915, a German submarine sank the British passenger liner *Lusitania* near the coast of Ireland. Among the approximately 1,200 passengers killed were 128 Americans. The following

TORPEDOED BY A GERMAN SUBMARINE, THE *LUSITANIA* SANK IN FIFTEEN MINUTES, TAKING MORE THAN A THOUSAND MEN, WOMEN, AND CHILDREN TO THEIR DEATHS.

spring the French liner *Sussex* was sunk and several Americans lost their lives. As the war continued and the Germans became increasingly desperate, they announced they would attack American ships suspected of carrying supplies for the Allies. Many ships were sunk and many lives were lost.

Meanwhile, German and Austrian agents planted bombs in American depots and shipyards to keep American goods from reaching the Allies. In the most spectacular of these attacks, on July 30, 1916, two powerful explosions ripped through a munitions transfer depot on Black Tom Island in New York harbor, shattering windowpanes for twenty-five miles around and killing seven people. The explosion even gouged holes in the Statue of Liberty.

Then, in early 1917, a message that had been sent by the German foreign minister Arthur Zimmermann to the German ambassador in Mexico was made public. In the "Zimmermann telegram," the foreign minister instructed the ambassador to invite the president of Mexico to join with Germany, should the United States enter the war. Germany promised Mexico financial assistance to "reconquer" the states of Texas, New Mexico, and Arizona. Americans were outraged.

As war fever took hold in the United States, the British did their best to help it along. They enlisted well-known writers, including Rudyard Kipling, Thomas Hardy, and Arthur Conan Doyle—creator of Sherlock Holmes—to promote the Allied cause. Their propaganda was very effective. Ellen Geer Sangster, who was eighteen when the war broke out, wrote many years later about how she saw the Germans: "Of course, like most of my contemporaries I swallowed fish hook and sinker all the horror stories about German atrocities, and it took me a long time after the war before I could consider a German altogether human."

Many supported the British cause because they had British ancestors or simply because they identified with the English-speaking British people. There was also widespread sympathy for the French. Many Americans, recalling that the French had come to the aid of the colonists during the American Revolution, believed that the United States had a debt to repay. This sentiment was voiced eloquently when the first U.S. troops arrived in France and marched through Paris. "Lafayette, we are here!" an American officer exclaimed, thinking back to the French general who served at Washington's side in the Revolution. His words were immediately taken as a pledge of American solidarity.

Even before entering the war, the United States was profiting from it, mainly through business with the Allies. By 1916, two years into the conflict, Americans had sold more than one billion dollars' worth of weapons to the Allies, as well as wheat, corn, processed food, machinery, and pharmaceuticals. U.S. banks were making huge loans. By the war's end, they would have loaned the Allies more than ten billion dollars. These loans boosted the U.S. economy because the Allies used most of the money to buy American products.

Building an Army

In April 1917 news that the Americans were joining the Allies probably did not make German military experts tremble. Far from being a major power, the U.S. Army ranked seventeenth in the world in terms of size, consisting of barely 100,000 men. In addition, there were about 132,000 men in the National Guard, but these were generally part-time soldiers, poorly trained. There was not a single regular division (a unit of 28,000 men) prepared for combat in Europe. It was clear that drastic measures had to be taken.

One of the astonishing facts of World War I was that, during the nineteen months of U.S. involvement, Americans raised an army and navy of more than four million people. But in order to create a fighting force out of virtually nothing, the U.S. government

THE ARMY MADE IT EASIER FOR MEN TO ENLIST BY BRINGING MOBILE RECRUITING STATIONS TO THEM, SUCH AS THIS ONE, SET UP IN DOWNTOWN NEW YORK CITY.

had to take steps that not everyone approved.

One of these steps was enacting a draft. On May 18, 1917, President Wilson signed into law the Selective Service Act, requiring all males between the ages of twenty-one and thirty to register for military service. More than 10 million men registered. The age limits were later extended to include men aged eighteen to forty-five, and by the war's end, more than 24 million—44 percent of American males—had registered.

Men who registered were given lottery numbers. All the

numbers were put in a glass bowl, and Newton D. Baker, the secretary of war, pulled out the numbers of the men who were to report for duty first. More than 2.8 million men were drafted into the army during the course of the war. Other men enlisted, or enrolled voluntarily.

Some people, including former president Teddy Roosevelt, were enthusiastic supporters of the draft. Roosevelt believed that military training would help unify a country made up of many nationalities and cultures. "The military tent where they all sleep side by side," he said, "will rank next to the public school among the great agents of democratization."

IN A LOTTERY HELD LATER IN THE WAR, VICE PRESIDENT THOMAS R. MARSHALL DRAWS THE NUMBERS OF THE MEN WHO WERE TO REPORT FOR DUTY.

Private Joseph Gaffney, from New York City, was one young man who seemed to have experienced the "democratization" Teddy Roosevelt hoped for. In this letter to his father he describes the many different kinds of men he met in the camp in Massachusetts where he was in training, waiting to leave for France.

Camp Devens
Ayer, Mass.
Jan. 18, 1918

Dear Father,

I am beginning to get acquainted with this place now. . . .

The Twenty-ninth is a "Rainbow" regiment. In our building . . . there are fellows from almost every state in the Union. On one side of me is Buford Smith of Kentucky, on the other Bill Starcher of Frisco. At my head a fellow from Indiana and at my feet a fellow from Kansas. This morning in the rubbish box there were papers from Boston, Louisville, Santa Fe, Seattle and Hartford. . . .

This morning, I overheard a bunch of fellows arguing as to which was the most progressive city in the country. Each one had a different city: St. Paul, Milwaukee, Denver, Seattle, Santa Fe and others. I chimed in with Bronx, which, of course, settled the matter. . . .

I haven't heard from any of my friends yet and you can bet I will be glad when I receive the first letter from home.

With love for all, I am
Your loving son

Joe

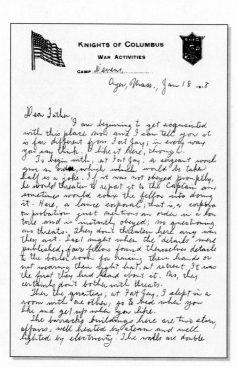

"Our Service Flag"

In high schools all over the country, students and teachers volunteered for military service. Langston Hughes, who would one day become a famous poet and a leading figure in the Harlem Renaissance cultural revival of the 1920s, was a high-school student in Cleveland, Ohio, during the war. He wrote this poem for the March 1918 issue of the Central High School *Monthly*, his school newspaper.

Our Service Flag

Central's heart has a memory
That will live for many a day:
A memory full of glorious pride,
For our boys who have gone away—
Pride for those boys who closed the book
Of Latin or History's lore,
And went to the army camps to work
On the greater task of war.
So Central unfurls her Service Flag,
Blue stars on a field of white,
To show that the school can never forget
Those boys who have gone to fight.
Oh, Central is proud of her soldiers
Who march in the ranks today,
And the heart of the old school is with them,
Our boys who have gone away.

"Hyphenated Americans"

Incidents such as the sinking of the *Lusitania* and the publication of the Zimmermann telegram had helped push American public opinion toward war. Nevertheless, not everyone was eager to join the fight. The United States was a nation of immigrants, and many citizens still had ties to countries that were now the enemy.

In 1917 more than eight million Americans considered Germany their country of origin, because either they or their ancestors had been born there. Many German Americans lived in close-knit communities where they retained German customs. Many spoke German and read German-language newspapers. German Americans had been one of the most influential ethnic groups in the United States, but suddenly they were under suspicion.

Another group suspected of having loyalties to the enemy was the Irish Americans. As part of Great Britain, Ireland was officially one of the Allies. However, the Irish had long chafed under British rule, and many Irish Americans hoped to see Great Britain defeated in the war.

Jewish Americans also sympathized with the Germans in the early years of the war. Germany was seen as relatively friendly to Jews, and some German Jews enjoyed positions of high social and economic status. Many Jewish Americans considered Russia, not Germany, the enemy. Since the end of the nineteenth century, Jews in Russia had suffered under pogroms—government-sponsored attacks on Jewish villages. Many Jews had fled Russia and immigrated to the United States or Palestine (modern-day Israel).

When the U.S. declared war, there was much talk about "hyphenated Americans" and what could be done to ensure their loyalty, to get every American behind the war effort.

Winning American Minds

President Wilson recognized that waging war required the support of all the people. "It is not an army we must shape and train for war, it is a nation," he said. The president believed that if citizens were educated to understand the war, they would pull together to win it. To educate the public—and this had to be done with lightning speed once war was declared—Wilson created the Committee

on Public Information (CPI). George Creel was appointed to head the committee. Creel was a journalist and an ardent reformer who had worked on Wilson's election campaigns. He believed that the committee should focus on "big, ringing statements," on rousing patriotism rather than censoring the opposition.

Creel recruited journalists, psychologists, advertising executives, artists, writers, scholars, and even movie directors to bring Americans together behind the war. Posters appeared everywhere, urging people to enlist in the army, join the Red Cross, write cheerful letters to servicemen.

Local leaders all over the country—75,000 of them—were recruited to give short patriotic speeches, with the texts supplied by the CPI. These "Four-Minute Men" would deliver their messages in movie theaters, while the film reels were being changed, and in many other public places.

I<small>N A LETTER TO HER BROTHER JOE, FLORRIE GAFFNEY, A TEACHER, DESCRIBES A TYPICAL DAY ON THE HOMEFRONT, WHERE EVERYONE, IT SEEMED, WAS BECOMING INVOLVED IN THE WAR EFFORT. JOE WAS STILL IN CAMP DEVENS, MASSACHUSETTS.</small>

Thursday
[14 March 1918]

Dear Joe:

. . . Nothing like breaking up the monotony of daily routine! Next week there is no school in the mornings. Instead all the teachers go to various auditoriums to hear some patriotic speeches to be given by famous orators. I heard a speech last week by a Mr. McElroy who succeeded Pres. Wilson as professor of Hist[ory] in Princeton. He was wonderful! I hope next week's talkers will be as good.

Mother is at a euchre [a card game to raise money] for the Red Cross in the Fordham Club. Kittie is with her. I hope they win something, just for the excitement of it.

Anna has got suddenly ambitious & is in playing the piano, which reminds me that "My Heart is in the Trenches" is now quite popular on Grand Avenue. . . .

Lots of love from all

Florrie

AT A TIME BEFORE RADIO AND TELEVISION, THE "FOUR-MINUTE MEN" BROUGHT NEWS
OF THE WAR TO EVERY CORNER OF THE COUNTRY. POSTERS LIKE THIS ONE ALSO HELPED
THE GOVERNMENT GET PEOPLE BEHIND THE WAR EFFORT.

The CPI's program included study plans for elementary schools. Teachers were to explain to their students that Americans were fighting to protect the French, who had been attacked by the Germans, and to "keep the German soldiers from coming to our country and treating us the same way." Older students were to be taught the differences between the German government, with its unlimited powers, and the democratic American system.

Mobilizing for Victory

To make sure that U.S. manufacturers cooperated in producing the materials needed for the war, President Wilson created the War Industries Board. In March 1918 the president appointed Bernard M. Baruch, a successful Wall Street investor, to head the WIB.

The WIB had to determine what was needed—both on the homefront and for the war effort—and make sure factories produced it. Automobile manufacturers at first wanted to continue producing automobiles for the civilian market, and they resisted demands to start building trucks and tanks for the army. But the WIB controlled where the raw materials went. "You won't get your steel; that is all," Baruch threatened the automakers. They shifted production to the needed war machines.

A shortage of weapons was a major problem. U.S. factories had to struggle to produce enough guns and ammunition to outfit the new army. Often weapons were not manufactured fast enough to allow recruits to practice with them before they were sent to the front. Leo J. Bailed, a private with the Ninth Infantry, who arrived in France in September 1917, recalled that he, like the rest of his company, had never fired a Springfield rifle. In fact, few in his company had ever fired any firearm. "We were woefully ignorant of the basic principles of a soldier," he later wrote.

LIKE LEO BAILED, PRIVATE GAFFNEY FOUND HE HAD MUCH TO LEARN ABOUT SOLDIER-ING. HE WAS NOT HANDED A RIFLE UNTIL FOUR MONTHS AFTER ARRIVING AT TRAINING CAMP. IN THIS LETTER HE TELLS OF HIS FIRST EXPERIENCE AT THE RIFLE RANGE.

Camp Devens, Mass.
Sunday, May 19, 1918

Dear Mother,

First chance I've had to write, today, at 8:45 P.M. Just finished cleaning our guns after returning from the range. . . .

I suppose you will be interested in my first trip to the range. We had lunch at ten o'clock and reached the range at noon. I was one of the first to shoot. The biggest surprise I got was the "kick" of the gun. . . .

Not so bad [he scored 92 hits out of a possible 125], considering that I never handled a gun before. Richardson, who said that he was born with a gun in his hand, only made 97. I think mine is above the average. . . .

There was one surprising thing. I didn't mind the noise from my gun at all but the guns on either side came near lifting my hat off. I got more used to it, though, after a while.

After supper, then, we had to clean the guns and I can tell you they were dirty. Between dust and powder it took eight of us a good two hours to clean three of them. We got them clean though. Well, all things must end, even this, so Good Night.

Love & kisses to all

Joe

Through the WIB, the government took control of private businesses to an extent never before seen in the country. Resources could no longer be "wasted" on frivolous goods or nonessentials. Makers of corsets (close-fitting women's undergarments) were ordered to stop using metal for the stays that held the corsets rigid. Shoemakers were instructed to use less leather, and coffin makers were not to use brass, bronze, or copper in the caskets they built. Women's skirts were shortened to use less cloth. To cut down on waste, manufacturers were told to standardize: to make fewer different sizes of plows, fewer colors of typewriter ribbons, fewer styles of baby carriages.

Everything did not always run smoothly. The winter of 1917–1918 was especially cold, and the Fuel Administration could not get coal mine owners to agree on prices and deliveries. To make matters worse, snow and freezing weather closed down the railroad lines. Coal cars sat in rail yards, leaving homes and businesses without fuel. Barges carrying loads of coal were stuck in the ice on major rivers and the Great Lakes. Many factories had to shut down during this fuel crisis, and "heatless days" were instituted to conserve coal. "Guess you have heard the latest on the coal situation," Marie Tice wrote to her brother, Joe Gaffney, in January 1918. "A legal holiday every Monday . . . and a complete Industrial shut down for five days beginning Saturday." Joe's Aunt Lolie wrote, "You should see good old New York by night, darkness on all sides—and every store closed." Joe's father described having little heat in his apartment building, no power for the elevator, and "all the saloons had no heat & most other stores all closed at 5 P.M."

In the spring of 1918, Americans set their clocks ahead one hour as daylight saving time was adopted. The new program was meant to conserve fuel by bringing work hours in line with the hours of daylight. The time change was confusing at first. "I suppose the camp clocks will be moved forward with those of the rest of the country," Florrie Gaffney wrote to Joe. "Mother is so afraid that the church clocks won't be changed and she'll be going to Mass when there is none."

"Blood or Bread"

Food production and distribution had to be carefully organized and controlled once the United States entered the war. American farms were already feeding the Allies; feeding the army would put a greater strain on the food supply. In May 1917 President Wilson established the Food Administration and appointed future president Herbert Hoover to head it.

Hoover was already a hero. He was an American success story, a hardworking self-made man. Orphaned at the age of nine, educated as an engineer at Stanford University, he had made a fortune in various mining businesses. He had been in Europe when the war broke out and had quickly started organizing efforts to feed starving civilians in occupied areas of France and Belgium. Back in the United States, as head of the Food Administration, he proclaimed that his agency would not require Americans to ration their food as Europeans were doing, but instead would "mobilize the spirit of self-denial and self-sacrifice in this country." He would not demand sacrifices; he would ask for them.

Food supplies could be increased in two ways, Hoover reasoned: by increasing production and by decreasing what people on the homefront consumed. Increased production meant that more hands were needed to work the farms. This was doubly difficult because many men who might have farmed were now in the army. High-school boys were recruited to work on farms, and before the war ended, young women were also called to help in the fields.

Helen J. Miller joined the Woman's Land Army of America in 1918 and wrote of marching off to farms, vegetable gardens, and greenhouses near her home to work as a "farmerette." Farmerettes, who had to be at least seventeen years old, were outfitted in uniforms and straw hats. Most of the employers were very friendly, Helen recalled, and some invited the women to enjoy their lunch, which they brought along in baskets, on the front porch. Most of these young women had never worked outside their homes before, and this experience gave them a measure of independence and a view of life beyond their doors.

The Food Administration also encouraged citizens to plant "victory gardens" in their yards or in vacant lots. Even the White House lawn was the site of a victory garden, and President Wilson did not stop at that in setting an example for ingenuity. He brought in a flock of sheep to keep the grass trimmed, freeing the White House gardeners to work elsewhere. The sheep kept the lawn neat and produced wool that was auctioned off by the Red Cross, raising almost $100,000 for that organization's war work.

To inspire Americans to conserve food, Hoover's agency produced posters with hard-hitting messages. "Blood or Bread," read one poster. "Others are giving their blood. You will shorten the war—save life if you eat only what you need and waste nothing." "Be patriotic to the core," another poster urged, encouraging people to get every last bite out of the fruit they ate. Civilians were asked to "serve the cause of freedom" by observing wheatless Mondays, meatless Tuesdays, and porkless Saturdays; by substituting corn

THESE HIGH-SCHOOL "FARMERETTES" TEND THEIR WAR GARDEN, PLANTED BEHIND A PUBLIC LIBRARY.

for wheat; and by eating fish or beans instead of meat. Conserving food—a patriotic effort that came to be known as Hooverizing, after the Food Administration's famous director—became a way of life for many Americans.

Despite the sacrifices, Joe Gaffney's cousin Agnes managed to keep her sense of humor. Here she writes to Joe about how the war was affecting her life.

242 East 50th St.
N.Y., Feb. 8, '18.

Dear Joey,

How goes Camp Devens? I hear you've left the "Life of Riley" for the "Life-of-One-of-a-Mob." Well, there's no accounting for taste but I'm glad you like it better.

Now—I['m] sorry to say—Joe—that this epistle will be neither

A. Long

1. Because I only own a few of these cards.

2. Because paper is so far skyward that a poor schoolma'am cannot reach it.

B. Nor Interesting

1. Because my brain has been frozen along with the gas and water.

(a) When a hard thing freezes it takes some time for it to thaw.

You see, these heatless, wheatless, eatless, gasless, waterless, moneyless days have got me going so after this I shall write in outline form for I suppose a spaceless letter will come next.

There is nothing new around here except a little less weather these last two days. In fact—yesterday was so very mild that it made one think of twittering leaves and budding birds. The children all had the Spring Fever and I could see in their eyes that they were joining their teacher in counting the days to vacation. It made me forget all at once the days that we have just lived through—when we sat around one measley little candle—clad in our overcoats— and imported our breakfast—all ready made—from the bakery shop. Some winter we've had! What say you natives of Camp Devens???

. . . The entire family wish to be remembered and they all join me in wishing you Good Luck.

Sincerely, Agnes E. H.

Liberty Bonds

War is an expensive proposition and this one was to cost far more than any of America's previous wars. In the two years following its entry into the war, the United States spent more than $31 billion, including loans to the Allies. In five years, from 1915 to 1920, the national debt grew from $1 billion to $20 billion.

In 1917 and 1918 Revenue Acts were passed, the first time in the history of the United States that income was taxed substantially. These laws taxed profits earned by businesses and income earned by individuals. Taxes paid for about one-third of the cost of the war.

To pay the rest of the bill, the government borrowed from banks and wealthy investors and also from ordinary citizens, who could lend the government money by buying bonds. A person might buy a bond for $50, for example, and then in thirty years, cash in the bond and get $150 back. The $100 difference would be the interest the government paid for the use of the bond buyer's money. Bonds offered to ordinary citizens were called Liberty Bonds. They cost $50 and up. People with less money to invest could

POSTER ARTISTS USED IMAGES THAT TUGGED AT THE HEARTSTRINGS TO CONVINCE PEOPLE TO BUY LIBERTY BONDS.

For Home and Country

VICTORY LIBERTY LOAN

A WORKER AT A PRINTING PRESS DISPLAYS AN ISSUE OF LIBERTY BONDS.

buy War Savings Certificates for $5, and even schoolchildren could join in by buying twenty-five-cent Thrift Stamps. A major publicity campaign was launched to get people to buy bonds. Posters urged, "Beat Back the Hun with Liberty Bonds," and "Lick a Stamp and Lick the Kaiser." (A Hun was a German soldier; the kaiser, Germany's ruler.) More than $21 billion was raised for the war effort though the Liberty Bond program.

Bond campaigns not only raised money but also helped build homefront support for the war. Businesses and social clubs sponsored competitions to see who could sell the most bonds. Employers gave their workers time off to attend huge Liberty Bond rallies hosted by famous movie stars such as Charlie Chaplin,

Mary Pickford, and Douglas Fairbanks. Opera star Enrico Caruso lent his legendary voice to rallies, as did vaudeville performer Al Jolson, who would later appear in the first "talking movie," *The Jazz Singer*. Celebrity appearances like these drew huge crowds of eager fans and were later replayed for audiences in movie theaters all across the country.

FLORRIE GAFFNEY DESCRIBED A DAY OF LIBERTY BOND ACTIVITIES IN A LETTER TO HER BROTHER, JOE.

[30 Apr. 1918]
Tuesday 6:30 P.M.

Dear Joe:

Just read your letter. It's great to have your company picture. We look up all the ones whose names you mention and feel as if we know them. . . .

There was a wonderful Liberty Loan Parade on Friday. We got the P.M. [afternoon] off and stood from 2:30 till 6:30 watching it. The women marchers made a big hit.

New York is behind in the Loan according to the reports,—but I can't believe it—Our New York! In school I sold 51 bonds amounting to $4800. We had a rally on Webster Ave and 198 St. on Sat. night and you never heard such thrilling talks as those children gave. They were wonderful. Judge Morris spoke too but in no way outshone the children. We sold $3500 in bonds and 400 Thrift Stamps.

One clever stunt in the line of devices for getting bonds by original ways was performed by a man on the Concourse and Fordham Road. He climbed up to the Fire escape and rapped on the window for the people to come out and buy bonds. They came & then he continued his climb until he had everyone out on the fire-escapes and a few hundred on the street. He sold quite a few bonds. . . .

The hard working part of the family will soon be home so I will get back to my post on K.P. [Kitchen Patrol]

Lots of love & kisses
Florrie

Did you get your picture taken yet.

Transatlantic Mail

In 1917 most of the mail within the United States was carried by train. Airmail routes were not set up until May 1918, and then they covered only short distances between a handful of cities. Letters usually took two or three days to arrive.

Mail to and from Europe was a different story. No one had yet crossed the Atlantic in an airplane, and it would be decades before transatlantic mail was regularly carried by air. In 1918 overseas mail was carried by ship and it took weeks for letters to arrive.

Soldiers departing for overseas duty were not allowed to write telling their families when they were scheduled to sail. The government feared that if word got out a German submarine might be waiting for the American ships. Thus families could not know for sure when their loved ones had left for Europe. The government did provide a postcard that the men could fill out and drop in a mail pouch as they boarded their ships. Families waited anxiously until the safe-arrival postcard appeared. In New York, the family of Private Joseph Gaffney waited nearly six weeks for this card from France.

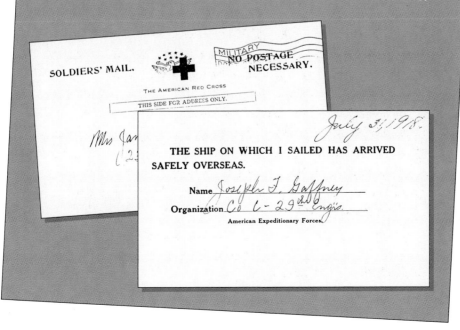

2

INTOLERANCE

Once lead this people into war, and they'll forget there ever was such a thing as tolerance. To fight you must be brutal and ruthless, and the spirit of ruthless brutality will enter into the very fiber of our national life, infecting Congress, the courts, the policeman on the beat, the man in the street.

—PRESIDENT WOODROW WILSON, 1917

President Wilson spoke these words to a friend a few days before asking Congress to declare war on Germany. The president was worried because he understood that once the United States entered the war, life on the homefront would change. There would be little room for discussion or exchange of ideas. The country would have to become a single voice supporting the war. Those who disagreed would be silenced.

President Wilson was right. U.S. entry into the World War brought with it an era of intolerance—lack of respect for the opinions and ideas of others—that makes for shocking reading today.

Speaking Out against the War

The First Amendment to the Constitution of the United States, adopted in 1791 as part of the Bill of Rights, promises the right to speak freely. The amendment guarantees that "Congress shall make no law . . . abridging the freedom of speech, or of the press." Despite these guarantees, during World War I government leaders believed that freedom of speech could harm the war effort. In 1917 and 1918 four laws were passed that seriously restricted free speech.

The Espionage Act, passed in June 1917, prohibited spying and sabotage, and forbade public criticism of the military. The

UNDER THE NEW LAWS, ALIENS, PEOPLE WHO WERE NOT U.S. CITIZENS, HAD TO RE-GISTER AND BE FINGERPRINTED SO THE GOVERNMENT COULD KEEP TRACK OF THEM.

Trading with the Enemy Act, also passed in 1917, made it illegal to do business with Germany and, later, with Austria-Hungary. The law also allowed the postmaster general to decide which publications could be sent through the mail. Once this law was passed, many organizations that opposed the war could no longer use the postal service to distribute their materials. The Alien Act of 1918 allowed the deportation of noncitizens who were suspected of actions and beliefs hostile to the government, such as advocating violent revolution. The Sedition Act, also passed in 1918, banned "uttering, printing, writing, or publishing any disloyal, profane, scurrilous, or abusive language" against the government or the armed forces.

More than three thousand Americans were prosecuted by the Justice Department under the Espionage and Sedition Acts. Many of these people were prosecuted for opposing the draft. Some objected to the very idea of conscription—another word for the draft—believing it violated their liberties under the Constitution. Others simply wanted nothing to do with militarism of any kind.

One person who spoke out was Emma Goldman, a radical political activist who had emigrated from Russia to the United States in 1885. Goldman organized the No-Conscription League in New York, and within two weeks more than eight thousand men had signed a pledge not to register for the draft. She spoke with passionate conviction: "We, who came from Europe, came here looking to America as the promised land. I came believing that liberty was a fact. And when we today resent war and conscription, it is not that we are foreigners and don't care, it is precisely because we love America and we are opposed to war."

Government authorities considered Goldman "the most dangerous woman in America." She was arrested, convicted of violating the Espionage Act, fined ten thousand dollars, and sentenced to two years in prison. In 1919 she was deported to Russia.

EMMA GOLDMAN GIVES AN IMPASSIONED SPEECH TO A CROWD IN NEW YORK CITY.

Like Emma Goldman, Louise Olivereau also spoke out against the war. Olivereau was an anar-chist and a pacifist who worked for the Industrial Workers of the World, a radical labor union, in Seattle. She wrote and mailed out leaflets protesting the draft, paying for them herself. Olivereau was arrested under the Espionage Act and sent to prison. In this letter, written after the war, her friends plead her case to the U.S. Attorney General.

5163rd Ave. West,
Seattle Wash.
April, 12, 1919.
A. Mitchel[l] Palmer,
The Honorable, Attorney General
Washington, D. C.

Dear Sir:

We understand that you have announced your intentions of reviewing all the cases of Conscientious Objectors, Military prisoners, and those who opposed the Government in its war policy, purely on humanitarian grounds, and not through any symp[a]thy with the Central Powers.

We wish to call to your attention the case of Louise Olivereau, who was convicted and sentenced under the Esp[i]onage act, in this District December 3, 1917, to serve a sentence of 10 years at Canon City, Colorado, where she has been confined for the past 16 months.

Miss Olivereau is an American girl born of French parents. She is a very intelligent woman, of an exceedingly sensitive and artistic nature. She has since early girlhood consistently opposed all forms of violence. Prison life is going very hard with her, because she was a child of the great out doors.

We consider Miss Olivereau's a very excessive sentence. And those of us who know her, feel that she has served quite enough time, and received sufficient punishment; that she should be released immediately, now, that the war is over. We do not believe that it should be our goal, as American citizens to imprison those who disagree with us Politically to the extent of destroying their health and crushing their life.

Therefore, Mr. Palmer, we ask, you to use your power to liberate our friend Louise Olivereau, before it is too late, that she may again walk in the open air and sun, and enjoy the privilege of earning her own living.

We are yours very truly,
Minnie Parkhurst and Sarah Cahen

L OUISE OLIVEREAU'S CASE WAS REVIEWED AND SHE WAS SET FREE. AS SHE PREPARED TO LEAVE THE COLORADO STATE PENITENTIARY, SHE WROTE TO HER FRIEND MINNIE.

March 22, 1920

My dear Minnie:

. . . I've got everything finished now, even my cell almost emptied of boxes & books &c, and it begins really to feel like moving-time. You know the idea of leaving has been fantastically unreal all this time—just as when I was a child & was told I should sometime go to Heaven & see the saints & the angels. I believed that I should; and, more recently, I have believed I should go home—but home & heaven have seemed almost equally remote & unreal. When I get outside and can turn around & look in at myself, I shall set down some of the curious mental experiences & processes I have undergone here for your information & entertainment. . . .

What is the use of going on with this letter when I shall see you so soon! . . . Meanwhile, my love goes ahead of me, to you & all the family.

Eager for the day of Universal Freedom.

Louise Olivereau

LOUISE OLIVEREAU RETURNED HOME AND RESUMED HER POLITICAL ACTIVITIES: DISTRIBUTING PAMPHLETS, WORKING TO IMPROVE PRISON CONDITIONS, ORGANIZING SUPPORT FOR OTHER POLITICAL PRISONERS, AND WORKING WITH LABOR UNIONS.

Silencing the Critics

Government posters encouraged Americans to report anyone who appeared disloyal. A person spreading pessimistic stories about the progress of the war or giving or asking for confidential military information was immediately suspect. Be on the alert, citizens were told, for anyone who "crie[s] for peace, or belittle[s] our

Baseball and the War

What were professional baseball players supposed to do when other able-bodied men were enlisting or being drafted to fight? At first, baseball club owners went on with "business as usual" and their teams played ball. But the owners were roundly criticized. They tried making the argument that baseball was an "essential industry" and that players should be exempt from the draft. But Secretary of War Newton Baker would have none of that. He ruled that "players in the draft age must obtain employment calculated to aid in the successful prosecution of the war or shoulder guns and fight."

Many ballplayers found jobs in war industries. More than two hundred went to war, among them Ty Cobb, Hank Gowdy, and Grover Cleveland Alexander. Three were killed in action, including Eddie Grant, former captain of the New York Giants.

Today baseball games and other sporting events begin with a show of patriotism that dates from the last weeks of World War I. In the fall of 1918, American soldiers in France were preparing for a battle that would end up deciding the war—the battle to push back the Germans at Saint-Mihiel. Back home, the Chicago Cubs and the Boston Red Sox were playing the first game of the World Series at Comiskey Park in Chicago. The seventh inning came and the fans rose for the stretch. This is what happened next, as described in the *New York Times* the next day:

As the crowd of 19,274 spectators . . . stood up to take the afternoon yawn the band broke forth to the strains of The Star-Spangled Banner.

The yawn was checked and heads were bared as the ball players turned quickly about and faced the music. . . . First the song was taken up by a few, then others joined, and when the final notes came, a great volume of melody rolled across the field. It was at the very end that the onlookers exploded into thunderous applause and rent the air with a cheer that marked the highest point of today's enthusiasm.

The song was played at every remaining game of the World Series, marking the start of a baseball tradition. "The Star-Spangled Banner" was officially adopted as the national anthem in 1931.

GROVER CLEVELAND ALEXANDER, ONE OF BASEBALL'S GREATEST PITCHERS EVER,
SERVED IN THE TRENCHES OF FRANCE AND CAME HOME SHELL-SHOCKED, NEARLY
DEAF, AND SUFFERING FROM EPILEPTIC SEIZURES AND ALCOHOLISM.

efforts to win the war." By the summer of 1918, the U.S. attorney general was receiving 1,500 letters a day, each accusing someone—a neighbor, a business acquaintance, sometimes even a relative—of speaking or acting against the government.

Volunteer groups, made up of citizens on the lookout for spies and sedition, sprang up across the country. The American Protective League was one of these groups, and it had a role in one of the most famous cases of the era. The case involved Eugene Debs, who had run for president on the Socialist Party ticket in 1912.

Most Socialists opposed the war, calling it a capitalist battle that would bring nothing but death and misery to the workers of the world. Socialists believed that wealth and economic power should be controlled by workers, not by bankers and investors. Conditions in the United States in the years before the war—the growth of big business, a small minority of people becoming hugely wealthy while others suffered in poverty—had contributed to growing support for the Socialists' views. Their opposition to the war fell on receptive ears: in local elections in the fall of 1917, Socialist candidates received many more votes than they had in previous years. The government feared the growing influence of the party and watched its leaders closely.

In June 1918, Eugene Debs appeared at a Socialist convention in Canton, Ohio. He told the cheering crowd:

> *The master class has always declared the wars; the subject class has always fought the battles. The master class has had all to gain and nothing to lose; the subject class has nothing to gain and all to lose—especially their lives.*

Some members of the American Protective League infiltrated the convention, and one of them took down Debs's speech word for word. It was the primary evidence used when the Socialist leader was brought to trial later that year. Debs was found guilty of ridiculing the army and navy, and of criticizing the conduct and aims of the war. A ten-year prison sentence was his punishment. In 1920, while still in prison, Debs ran for president and received nearly one million votes.

German Americans and Wartime Frenzy

Loyalty and patriotism rose to a near fever pitch during World War I. Phrases such as "Absolute and Unqualified Loyalty to Our Country" and "100 Percent Americanism" were in the air, and anything vaguely foreign was viewed as a threat. In this atmosphere of fear and suspicion, German Americans were especially suspect. Historically, they made up a large part of the population. Approximately six million Americans were of Germany ancestry. An additional two and a half million German Americans were naturalized citizens—they had been born in Germany. About a half million were German aliens—noncitizens. When President Wilson invoked the Alien Enemies Act of 1798, which allowed imprisonment of dangerous aliens without a trial, 63 German aliens were seized immediately and another 1,200 arrested during the first year of U.S. participation in the war.

Not surprisingly, many German Americans tried to make themselves as inconspicuous as possible. Some went so far as to change their last names.

PRESIDENT WOODROW WILSON

Many Americans were eager to show their disapproval of everything German. The governor of Iowa banned the speaking of German in public places. School boards banned the teaching of the German language. New names were invented to disavow any link to things German: the German shepherd became a "police dog", hamburgers (named for the German city Hamburg) became "liberty sandwiches," and the German dish sauerkraut became "liberty cabbage."

The hysteria did not stop at that. Many cases were reported of German Americans being harassed. And in April 1918 Robert P. Prager of Collinsville, Illinois, was lynched. Prager, although German-born, had applied for U.S. citizenship as soon as the war broke out and had tried to enlist but was rejected because he was blind in one eye. He got into a dispute with a group of miners, who jeered at him, calling him an enemy spy. They managed to inflame a mob of about seventy-five men, who descended on Prager's house, pulled him outside, stripped him and wrapped him in an American flag, then dragged him barefoot and stumbling through the streets. After the police pried Prager from the mob, the men forced their way into the police station, seized him again, and took him to the outskirts of town. There they hanged him before a cheering crowd of five hundred "patriots."

The mob's leaders, wearing red, white, and blue ribbons, were put on trial. Their defense was that theirs was a "patriotic murder." After twenty-five minutes of deliberation, the jury returned a verdict of not guilty. One of the jury members shouted, "Well, I guess nobody can say we aren't loyal now."

Some Americans considered everything German the enemy, including German culture. People in the music world were particularly affected. Many singers were forced to eliminate German songs from their programs. Some singers of German heritage were denied halls in which to perform. The Swiss-born conductor of the Boston Symphony (whose name was German) lost his job.

GERMAN HYSTERIA WAS SO RAMPANT THAT MUSICIANS WERE AFRAID TO PLAY MANY OF THE CLASSICS OF WESTERN MUSIC, BECAUSE THOSE PIECES HAPPENED TO HAVE BEEN COMPOSED BY GERMANS. LEOPOLD STOKOWSKI, A FAMOUS CONDUCTOR, WROTE TO PRESIDENT WILSON ON THIS ISSUE. ALTHOUGH HE SHOULD BE COMMENDED FOR RAISING THE PROBLEM TO WILSON, HIS LETTER MAY SEEM RATHER TIMID TO US TODAY.

August 20, 1918

My dear Mr. President:

It is with great hesitation that I approach you with regard to a problem now agitating the musical world. . . .

The question is—whether or not the music of the classical masters born in Germany during the eighteenth and nin[e]teenth centuries should be played in America during the war.

I fully endorse the elimination of German opera for the duration of the war (with the exception perhaps of certain works of Mozart which are so French or Italian in character as not really to come under the head of German opera). I also agree that it is necessary to eliminate both the German language and the works of living enemy composers from our concert stage. As a loyal citizen of the United States it is my desire and intention to do all that lies in my power for the good of my country and to do nothing prejudicial to its interests, but it is still a question in my mind whether it is for the good of the country to abolish a treasure of art which does not belong to Germany but to the world. . . .

As this question, however, is not really a musical one but a national one, I beg to submit it directly to the one in whose inspired guidance in all questions affecting the good of this country we can have the most complete confidence, namely to our President. If, in your opinion, it is necessary for the good of the nation that the music of Bach and Beethoven be abolished from our concert programs, it is needless to say that I shall unquestionably abide by your decision.

Please accept, Mr. President, my grateful appreciation of any consideration you may be willing to give to this matter, and believe me to be respectfully and faithfully yours,

Leopold Stokowski

PRESIDENT WILSON RESPONDED TO THIS LETTER, ADVISING MAESTRO STOKOWSKI TO BE GUIDED BY PUBLIC OPINION AND BY WHAT OTHER ORCHESTRAS WERE DOING.

3

AFRICAN AMERICANS AND THE GREAT WAR

If this is our country, then this is our war.

—W. E. B. DU BOIS,
AFRICAN-AMERICAN CIVIL RIGHTS
LEADER AND AUTHOR

*T*he Birth of a Nation

One of the most popular movies of the war years, seen by millions of eager viewers across the United States, was *The Birth of a Nation*. The film broke records for long runs and was seen by perhaps more people than any other film in history. It was so popular that President Wilson even arranged for it to be shown at the White House.

The movie was also controversial. It caused riots and arrests. It brought loud protests from groups such as the National Association for the Advancement of Colored People (NAACP), which renamed it *The Assassination of a Race*. For many people, the movie demonstrated that the United States still had a long way to go to free itself of racism.

The Birth of a Nation, originally titled *The Clansman*, was released in 1915, the fiftieth anniversary of the end of the Civil War. The

HOODED KU KLUX KLANSMEN IN A SCENE FROM *THE BIRTH OF A NATION.*

silent film epic tells a romanticized story of the South, covering the years before and during the Civil War and into Reconstruction. It contains battle scenes, special effects, and a cast of hundreds, making it an extravaganza the likes of which had never been seen before in an American movie. The villains of the story are greedy, leering blacks, some of whom are played by white actors in grotesque blackface. They threaten the "helpless whites"—as these characters are described in titles on the screen—whose lives have been destroyed by the defeat of the South. The "heroes" who come to the rescue are the night riders of the Ku Klux Klan.

The Birth of a Nation is still available on video. It is an astounding record of the state of race relations in the early part of the twentieth century.

Racism in the Military

Prejudice and discrimination against African Americans permeated American society in the early decades of the twentieth century. Often even the most highly educated and intelligent of white Americans did not question racism or protest against it. Segregation—separation of the races—was a given. These were laws requiring separate schools for blacks and whites, separate seating in public places, even separate drinking fountains and toilet facilities. These were known as Jim Crow laws, after a song-and-dance act performed in the 1800s by a white actor in blackface. Jim Crow was ingrained in southern life and was often a feature of northern life as well.

Segregation even reached into the armed services. Before war was declared in the United States, there were ten thousand African-American soldiers serving in segregated regiments in the U.S. Army. When the draft was instituted in 1917, blacks were enlisted along with whites. Black recruits were sent to training camps throughout the nation, with the War Department maintaining a ratio of at least two white recruits for each black. Two hundred thousand African-American soldiers went to France, where they served in segregated regiments. Most were assigned to menial positions, working as laborers or stevedores, loading and unloading ships.

Black leaders protested that their men were being excluded from combat, and in response General John Pershing, commander of U.S. forces in Europe, assigned some black units—among them the 369th Infantry Regiment—to fight alongside French forces.

AFRICAN-AMERICAN TROOPS ASSIGNED TO BUILD A RAILWAY LINE TO SUPPLY THE
FRONT LINES IN FRANCE

The French welcomed these reinforcements. The African Americans
fought valiantly, and the French recognized their extraordinary
bravery, awarding 170 medals to men of the 369th Infantry Regiment alone. Two black Americans, Privates Henry Johnson and

Needham Roberts, won the Croix de Guerre, or "Cross of War," France's highest military honor. They were the first Americans to be awarded that honor.

Black leaders lobbied strongly for the War Department to establish an officers' training camp for African Americans. While they bristled at the idea of a Jim Crow camp, they knew that a segregated camp was their only hope. "Our young men are so anxious to serve their country in this crisis that they are willing to accept a separate camp," wrote leaders of one African-American organization. "Fifteen hundred qualified men have already made application to such a camp." The camp was set up at Fort Des Moines, Iowa. In October 1917 it graduated a single class of 639 black officers, all assigned to serve under white commanding officers. The camp was then closed.

MEN OF THE 369TH INFANTRY REGIMENT CELEBRATE THE END OF THE WAR AT A PARTY IN NEW YORK IN EARLY 1919.

Jazz Goes to War

The men of the 369th Infantry not only fought bravely, they also left a cultural legacy to France. The regiment's band, led by James Reese Europe, a famous jazz musician, toured Europe in early 1918 and created a major stir with its music. The band rejoined the regiment for the Meuse-Argonne campaign later that year, a turning point of the war. The battle was a grueling struggle, and the 369th suffered heavy casualties. The war ended November 11, 1918, and the men came home in early 1919. Besides playing an important role in the liberation of France, the men of the 369th had brought jazz to France.

LIEUTENANT JAMES REESE EUROPE CONDUCTS THE RENOWNED 369TH REGIMENT BAND, THRILLING AMERICAN AND FRENCH AUDIENCES WITH THAT NEW AMERICAN MUSIC, JAZZ.

Lynchings: A Shameful Legacy

Racial violence was a part of the American scene and it became more intense during the war. Since the Civil War, lynching had been a very real fear for blacks in the South, and during the war years the number of lynchings increased.

Lynchings were horrifying events. A mob gathered and seized someone thought to have committed a "crime," sometimes nothing more than standing up to a white person, sometimes nothing at all. Victims—men and women—were seized in their own homes, or perhaps captured trying to flee, or even snatched out of jail. They were dragged by the mob to a spot, usually on the edge of town, where the victim was hanged from the branch of a tree. Sometimes people emptied their guns into the swaying body, sometimes they mutilated the body, and often the mob set the body on fire. Men brought their wives and children to participate and view the spectacle. Sightseers even came back the next day to revisit the scene or to look for "souvenirs."

Sometimes photographers recorded these scenes. Many of these photos have survived. Some were made into postcards, which whites could buy to send to African Americans as a warning or to give to friends or relatives, to boast of their attendance or participation. One of the most disturbing features of these photographs is the way members of the mob gaze directly into the camera, unashamed, sometimes even smiling. Needless to say, lynchings drove a wedge of deep distrust and hatred between blacks and whites.

IN 1917 THE NAACP HOLDS A PEACEFUL MARCH TO PROTEST LYNCHING.

AFRICAN-AMERICAN WRITERS, ESPECIALLY JOURNALIST IDA B. WELLS, WROTE, SPOKE OUT, AND ORGANIZED AGAINST LYNCHING. THE NAACP, WHICH WAS FOUNDED IN 1909, KEPT THE ISSUE IN THE NEWS AND ON THE CONSCIENCE OF WHITES. IN JUNE 1918 MEMBERS OF THE AFRICAN-AMERICAN PRESS AND OTHER DISTINGUISHED BLACK LEADERS SIGNED A PETITION AND PRESENTED IT TO PRESIDENT WILSON, URGING HIM TO TAKE ACTION AGAINST LYNCHING. THE PETITION, DRAFTED BY THE HARVARD-EDUCATED CIVIL RIGHTS LEADER W. E. B. DU BOIS, SPELLS OUT THE SHOCKING FACTS.

June 1918

IDA B. WELLS, THE JOURNALIST AND ANTI-LYNCHING CRUSADER

Address to the Committee on Public Information

We, the thirty-one representatives of the Negro press . . . and representatives of other racial activities, wish to affirm, first of all, our unalterable belief that the defeat of the German government and what it today represents is of paramount importance to the welfare of the world in general and to our people in particular.

We deem it hardly necessary, in view of the untarnished record of Negro Americans, to reaffirm our loyalty to Our Country and our readiness to make every sacrifice to win this war.

. . . We believe today that justifiable grievances of the colored people are producing not disloyalty, but an amount of unrest and bitterness. . . .

First and foremost among these grievances is lynching. Since the entrance of the United States in this war, 71 Negroes have been lynched, including four women, and over 178 have been victims of mob violence. The atrocities committed by American mobs during this time have been among the worst known to civilized life, and yet not a single person has been punished for lynching a Negro, nor have white mob leaders anywhere been brought to adequate justice.

The effect of these facts upon the Negro people has been indescribably depressing, and we earnestly believe, (and growing white and Southern opinion is coming to believe,) that Federal intervention to suppress lynching is imperative.

THE PRESIDENT RESPONDED POLITELY TO THE PETITION BUT DID NOTHING TO ADDRESS DIRECTLY THE ISSUE OF LYNCHING OR THE OTHER RACIAL PROBLEMS THE BLACK LEADERS LISTED.

Seeking Better Lives

The war years brought many changes to the American homefront, especially for African Americans. One of the major events of this era was the migration of large numbers of blacks from the South to northern cities. Hundreds of thousands of African Americans went north, where job opportunities had opened up.

When war broke out in Europe, demand for American goods was tremendous. The United States was one of the few countries that could produce the weapons, machinery, clothing, and food the warring countries needed. At first, U.S. factories sold to both sides of the conflict, although shipments to the Central Powers were hindered by the British naval blockade of the Atlantic. After the U.S. entered the war in 1917, those shipments, of course, stopped.

The naval blockade and fears of German submarine attacks made transatlantic travel dangerous, and few would-be immigrants from Europe were willing to risk making the journey. That meant that the steady stream of immigrants—the people American industry relied on as a source of cheap labor—slowed to a trickle. In addition, great numbers of men were leaving their jobs for military duty. American factories—most of them in the North—desperately needed more workers.

In the South many Americans, both black and white, were farmers. Even in the best of times, it was difficult for these people to earn a decent living. In 1915 and 1916 boll weevils ruined the cotton crop, plunging poor farmers even deeper into poverty. Meanwhile, news was circulating of well-paying jobs and better living conditions in the North. Many poor southerners decided to set off for the unknown. It is estimated that between 1910 and 1920, somewhere between 300,000 and 1,000,000 African Americans made their way north, with the greatest numbers migrating between 1916 and 1918.

For many black migrants, the North offered more than just the

A WORKER SETS THE TYPE FOR AN ISSUE OF THE *CHICAGO DEFENDER,* THE COUNTRY'S LARGEST BLACK-OWNED NEWSPAPER. THE NEWSPAPER URGED SOUTHERN BLACKS TO SEEK A BETTER LIFE IN NORTHERN CITIES.

hope of higher wages. It was also seen as a place where African Americans might be treated with the same respect as whites, where the law treated everyone fairly. The hopes and dreams of these Americans came out clearly in a report commissioned by the U.S. secretary of labor in 1917. Known as the Dillard study (after the director of the project), this report sought to explain the reasons behind the massive northern migration. W. T. B. Williams, the only African American among the government investigators, described his interviews with migrants during the summer of 1917:

> *I talked with all classes of colored people from Virginia to Louisiana—farm hands, tenants, farmers, hack drivers, porters, mechanics, barbers, merchants, insurance men, teachers, heads of schools, ministers, druggists, physicians, and lawyers—and in every instance the matter of treatment came to the front voluntarily. This is the all-absorbing, burning question among Negroes. For years no group of the thoughtful,*

intelligent class of Negroes, at any rate, have met for any purpose without finally drifting into some discussion of their treatment at the hands of white people.

Because Negroes have made few public complaints about their condition in the South, the average white man has assumed that they are satisfied; but there is a vast amount of dissatisfaction among them over their lot. . . . The Negro's list of grievances that have prepared him for this migration is a long one. . . .

There is a good deal in the statement of a leading colored woman of Florida: "Negroes are not so greatly disturbed about wages. They are tired of being treated as children; they want to be men."

The *Chicago Defender*, a newspaper with a mainly black readership, ran advertisements for jobs in northern cities. Many would-be migrants wrote to the newspaper, seeking advice and help. Emmett J. Scott, who had been appointed "special assistant for Negro affairs" by the War Department, collected these letters and published many of them in the *Journal of Negro History* in 1919. The letters provide a powerful and fascinating record of why southern blacks decided to pick up and move.

MANY FELT A SENSE OF DESPERATION.

Troy, Ala., Oct. 17, 1916.

Dear Sirs I am enclosing a clipping of a lynching again which speaks for itself. I do wish there could be sufficient pressure brought about to have federal investigation of such work. I wrote you a few days ago if you could furnish me with the addresses of some firms or co-opporations that needed common labor. So many of our people here are almost starving. The government is feeding [many and] quite a number here would go any where to better their conditions. If you can do any thing for us write me as early as posible.

MOST PEOPLE WROTE ABOUT JOB POSSIBILITIES. COMPANIES HOPING TO ATTRACT WORKERS SENT AGENTS TO PROVIDE RAILROAD PASSES FOR THE MIGRANTS, SINCE MOST COULD NOT AFFORD THE COST OF THE TRAIN TICKET.

Mobile, Ala., May 11, 1917

Dear sir and brother: on last Sunday I addressed you a letter asking you for information and I have received no answer. but we would like to know could 300 or 500 men and women get employment? and will the company or thoes that needs help send them a ticket or a pass and let them pay it back in weekly payments? We have men and women here in all lines of work we have organized a association to help them through you.

We are anxiously awaiting your reply

Jacksonville, Fla., May 5, 1917

Dear Sir: Kindly inform me by return mail are there any factories or concerns employing colored laborers, skilled or unskilled, the south is ringing with news from Chicago telling of the wonderful openings for colored people, and I am asking you to find the correct information whether I could get employment there or not. Please find postage enclosed for immediate reply.

Pensacola, Fla., April 21, 1917

Sir: You will please give us the names of firms where we can secure employment. Also please explain the Great Northern Drive for May 15th. We will come by the thousands. Some of us like farm work. The colored people will leave if you will assist them.

SOME PEOPLE WROTE OF THEIR HOPES OF PROVIDING A BETTER EDUCATION FOR THEIR CHILDREN.

Crescent, Okla., April 30, 1917

Sir: I am looking for a place to locate this fall as a farmer. Do you think you could place me on a farm to work on shares. I am a poor farmer and have not the money to buy but would be glad to work a mans farm for him. I am desirous of leaving here because of the school accommodations for children as I have five and want to educate them the best I can. Perhaps you can find me a position of some kind if so kindly let me know I will be ready to leave here this fall after the harvest is layed by. I am planting cotton.

E VEN TEENAGERS WERE WILLING TO LEAVE THEIR FAMILIES AND HOMES IN SEARCH OF A BETTER LIFE.

Selma, Alabama, May 19, 1917

Dear Sir: I am a reader of the Chicago Defender I think it is one of the Most Wonderful Papers of our race printed. Sirs I am writeing to see if You all will please get me a job. And Sir I can wash dishes, wash iron nursing work in groceries and dry good stores. Just any of these I can do. Sir who so ever you get the job from please tell them to send me a ticket and I will pay them. When I get their as I have not got enough money to pay my way. I am a girl of 17 years old and in the 8 grade at Knox Academy School. But on account of not having money enough I had to stop school. Sir I will thank you all with all my heart. May God bless you all. Please answer in return mail.

Palestine, Tex, Mar. 11th 1917

Sirs: this is somewhat a letter of information I am a colored Boy aged 15 years old and I am talented for an artist and I am in search of some one will Cultivate my talent I have studied Cartooning therefore I am a Cartoonist and I intend to visit Chicago this summer and I want to keep in touch with your association . . . from you[r] knowledge can a Colored boy be an artist and make a white man's salary up there[?] I will tell you more and also send a fiew samples of my work when I rec an answer from you.

"A Great Dark Tide"

Southern migrants were not always prepared for life in the northern cities. Discrimination, they found, did not end in the South.

CLEVELAND, OHIO, WITH ITS STEEL MILLS AND FACTORIES, DREW MANY AFRICAN AMERICANS. THE POET LANGSTON HUGHES WAS IN HIGH SCHOOL THERE AT THE TIME. IN *THE BIG SEA*, HIS AUTOBIOGRAPHY, HE DESCRIBES WHAT LIFE WAS LIKE FOR ONE BLACK FAMILY.

[My stepfather] was working in a steel mill during the war and making lots of money. But it was hard work, and he never looked the same afterwards. Every day he worked several hours overtime, because they paid well for overtime. But after a while, he couldn't stand the heat of the furnaces, so he got a job as caretaker of a theater building, and after that as janitor of an apartment house.

Rents were very high for colored people in Cleveland, and the Negro district was extremely crowded, because of the great migration. It was difficult to find a place to live. We always lived, during my high school years, either in an attic or a basement, and paid quite a lot for such inconvenient quarters. White people on the east side of the city were moving out of their frame houses and renting them to Negroes at double and triple the rents they could receive from others. An eight-room house with one bath would be cut up into apartments and five or six families crowded into it, each two-room kitchenette apartment renting for what the whole house had rented for before.

But Negroes were coming in in a great dark tide from the South, and they had to have some place to live. Sheds and garages and store fronts were turned into living quarters. As always, the white neighborhoods resented Negroes moving closer and closer—but when the whites did give way, they gave way at very profitable rentals. So most of the colored people's wages went for rent. The landlords and the banks made it difficult for them to buy houses, so they had to pay the exorbitant [unusually high] rents required. When my stepfather quit the steel mill job, my mother went out to work in service to help him meet expenses. She paid a woman four dollars a week to take care of my little brother while she worked as a maid.

Besides having to confront the difficulties of making ends meet, African Americans found that they had not left discrimination and

DURING A RACE RIOT IN CHICAGO IN JULY 1919, WHITES USE STONES TO ATTACK
RESIDENTS OF A BLACK GHETTO.

hatred behind. Racism was alive and well in the North, too. Some
whites felt threatened by the large numbers of newcomers, and
their simmering resentments sometimes exploded in violence and
race riots.

Riots frequently took the form of white mobs attacking
African Americans in city streets, or invading black neighborhoods,
destroying property and attacking people. African Americans
fought back, and there were many casualties on both sides,
although most of the dead were blacks. The violence was just
another sign of the deep-rooted hatred, fear, and distrust between
the races—a conflict that would continue to divide the nation for
decades after the Great War's end.

4

WOMEN'S WORK

[The rain was] cold and continuous, the mud like glue. . . . Our destination was Evacuation Hospital 11, where hundreds of seriously wounded men lay on the wet ground, waiting their turn for attention. . . . On a heavy night, three hundred or more wounded would be brought to us . . . . Fortunately, in all the mud and filth, there always seemed to be large packing cases of neatly folded gauze squares, large sponges and pads and other surgical dressings which had been put together with loving care by the women back home.

—NURSE ELIZABETH CAMPBELL BICKFORD,
SEPTEMBER 1918, NEAR VERDUN, FRANCE

A "Woman's Place"

As America entered World War I, women's lives were already quite different from the lives of their mothers. In 1915 writer Dorothy Dix described the "type of girl that the modern young man falls for" as a "husky young woman who can play golf all day and dance all night and drive a motor car, and give first aid to the injured if anybody gets hurt, and who is in no more danger of swooning than he is." Ads in magazines such as the *Ladies' Home Journal* showed young women with cropped hairdos, driving speedboats, their admiring boyfriends at their side.

WOMEN WORK AT MEN'S JOBS IN A MUNITIONS FACTORY.

The Great War would bring even greater challenges to traditional notions of a "woman's place" in society. The war demanded that Americans rethink their ideas of the kinds of work women could perform. Men were called away to military service and women took their places in factories and on farms. For the first time in U.S. history, women went on active duty in the armed services, usually as telephone operators, office workers, or nurses. Thousands of women served in Europe and on the homefront as volunteers with the American Red Cross, the YMCA, the Salvation Army, and other service organizations.

Many women hoped that these increased opportunities would continue after the war. After all, women were already demonstrating that they could do jobs people had assumed were for men only.

Women Reformers

Besides joining the workforce, women were also active in public life, especially in movements to improve social conditions. One leading reformer was Margaret Sanger, who opened the first birth control clinic, in 1916, in Brooklyn, New York, and who founded the National Birth Control League in 1921. Her goal was to help women plan their families and be more responsible for themselves.

Another leading reformer was Julia Lathrop. She was the first female director of a federal agency, the Children's Bureau, which was created in 1912. Its purpose was to improve the lives of moth-

MANY WOMEN JOINED THE RED CROSS AS VOLUNTEERS.

ers and their children. The war—and particularly the draft—had focused attention on the health of the country's young men, and the news was not good. About one-third of the men called in the first draft were rejected for physical defects. Lathrop argued that many of those health problems could have been corrected by better medical care in infancy and childhood.

"Saving babies is a vital part of fighting the war," Lathrop argued. She convinced President Wilson to declare the second year of the war as Children's Year, "a year in which, after all has been done for our men at the front . . . the civil population shall do all in its power to protect the children of this nation. . . ."

Then, as now, the major threat to a child's well-being was poverty. Lathrop called for the eradication of poverty: "If we decide that the abolition of poverty is a necessity of the democratic state, and not an unattainable luxury, then it can be accomplished in our own day, even in the throes of war." Some of the programs she advocated were enacted and still exist: assistance for families with dependent children, child labor laws that set the minimum age at which children can hold jobs and how many hours they may work, and regulations ensuring a safe milk supply. Some of Lathrop's other goals have not become reality: a minimum wage sufficient to support a family, prenatal (before birth) health care for all pregnant women, well-baby clinics for all infants, and adequate education for all children.

To carry out the programs of the Children's Bureau, an army of professionals was needed—doctors, teachers, public health nurses—as well as committed volunteers. Agencies of the bureau were set up in nearly every state. The overwhelming majority of these agencies were headed by women, and hundreds of other women were employed as public health nurses or staff members. So while the Children's Bureau sought to better the lives of mothers and their children, it also opened whole new fields of opportunity for working women.

The Right to Vote

American women had been fighting for the right to vote—suffrage—since the mid-nineteenth century. In the 1870 and 1880s, women in some states had secured "partial suffrages"—the right to vote in some local elections. By 1916 women in twelve states had full voting rights. But as America entered the Great War, women in most states still could not vote.

During the war, many American women felt an increasing urgency to make their voices heard. All over the country, women were attending meetings like the ones described in the following diary entries by young Ina Pihlman of Chatham, New Jersey:

June 29, 1915—Went to a suffragist meeting at Mrs. Ralph Lum's with Edna and Mrs. W. (Rose) Hamblen. A woman who had been at the Peace Conference at the Hague gave a very interesting talk on "The War and the Vote." Refreshments were served.

Sept. 17, 1915—Mother went to a suffrage meeting in the evening. She is especially interested because Finland, her native country (but she is an American citizen), was one of the first countries to give women the right to vote. (1906, I think.)

The struggles of suffragists did not go unrewarded. Soon after the war's end, in 1920, the Nineteenth Amendment to the Constitution finally gave women nationwide the right to vote.

MILITARY
NO POSTAGE
NECESSARY.

Brooklyn, New York
January 30, 1918

Dear Madam,

I read this mornings article in the New York American about the campaign to save babies. I fear my baby will be born too soon to have such wonderful help as you propose. My babies come fast and where I am going to meet the Doctors bills I cannot see. I have a daughter one year old this Jan. and we have had little else but Doctors bill[s] in the past 3 years. I cannot get enough bed clothing for that time without going in debt. I have a very good husband but he has such poor health. He makes 20.70 a week, but to buy coal at 30c a small bag and oil at 14c a gallon, and other things so high we can not save a penny. I dont like to tell my husband all I fear as he has enough to bear. My husband felt it is his duty to take out a Liberty Bond and we are paying for it 1.00 a week. I would like to ask him to give it up, but dont seem to be able to do so. I can and would gladly do sewing to earn some money but can find no work like that in these times. Can you show me a way out or a way I can help my self? I expect my baby the first of March. I hope I have not done anything wrong in writing to you like this. I am very respectfully.

Mrs. W. S.

The crowning achievement of the Children's Bureau was the Sheppard-Towner Maternity and Infancy Protection Act, passed in 1921. It was the first "women's bill" enacted after women won the right to vote in 1920. The act gave states matching funds from the federal government to help pay for public health nurses, clinics, and medical care for women in remote areas.

Women at War: "Yeomenettes" and "Lady Leathernecks"

In the spring of 1917, Secretary of the Navy Josephus Daniels made history. "Enroll women in the naval service as yeomen [clerks]," he proclaimed, "and we will have the best clerical assistance the country can provide." Thousands of women eagerly answered the call, becoming the first women in U.S. history to serve as official members of the military. Secretary Daniels not only believed that women could do men's work, but also thought they deserved salaries equal to men's. At the time, the idea of equal pay for equal work was revolutionary, and even today women sometimes must fight for fair salaries.

Women inducted into the navy worked in noncombat positions, such as radio electricians, pharmacists, chemists, accountants,

YEOMEN (F) AT THEIR POSTS IN A NAVAL STATION IN NEW ORLEANS

and telephone operators. "Free a Man to Fight" was the recruiting slogan. Newspapers christened the new recruits "yeomanettes," but Daniels objected: "I never did like this 'ette' business. I always thought if a woman does a job, she ought to have the name of the job." The navy women were officially called yeomen (F), with the F standing for "female."

Unlike the navy, the marines were in no hurry to enlist women. The first women marines were not inducted until August 1918, just a few months before the war ended. Responding to announcements that the marines were looking for "intelligent young women," eager applicants lined up outside recruiting offices. The requirements were so rigorous, though, that only 305 women were accepted. The recruits became privates in the Marine Corps Reserve and were signed up for four years of service. They received the same wages as men and were also paid living expenses, since there were no barracks for women.

ONE OF THE LUCKY FEW TO BE RECRUITED BY THE MARINES WAS MARTHA L. WILCHINSKI OF NEW YORK CITY. SHE WROTE TO HER SWEETHEART, BILL, TO TELL HIM THE EXCITING NEWS.

Dear Bill:

I've got the greatest news! No, I haven't thrown you over; I'm still strong for you, Bill. No, it's no use; don't try to guess. . . . Are you ready? Well, then,—I'm a lady leatherneck; I'm the last word in Hun hunters; I'm a real, live, honest-to-goodness Marine! . . .

But I'll begin from the beginning and tell you everything ad seriatim. That's Latin. It means, "Go to it, kid." You know I always had a kind of a hunch that the Marines would realize the necessity of women some day, so I was laying low and waiting. Well, when I heard they had at last hung out a sign at the recruiting station—"Women wanted for the United States Marine Corps"—I was ready. "Mother," says I, "give me your blessing, I'm going to be one of the first to enlist." I was there when the doors opened in the morning. I was one of the first all right—first six hundred! You'd think they were selling sugar or something. Well, when the crowd heard that you had to be willing to go anywhere as ordered and you had to be a crackerjack stenog, they thinned out some. And from what was left the lieutenant picked out twelve to go over to the colonel and have him give us the double O. I was one of them, of course. . . . He told us to report the next morning for a physical examination.

That was a terrible ordeal. It took three men and one woman to do the job. You can't appreciate what I went through. Those doctors must have thought I was a ventriloquist or a somnambulist or something. I had to cough through my nose and breathe through my ears. I had to stand on my right eyebrow and wave my left foot. . . .

Well, only three of us came out alive. The others had fallen by the wayside. Then the colonel came and told us to come over and be sworn in. . . . It was terribly impressive. Something kept sticking in my throat all the time. I don't know whether it was my heart or my liver. I had to swallow it several times before I could say, "I do." . . .

I hear some people are giving us nicknames. Isn't it funny the minute a girl becomes a regular fellow somebody always tries to queer it by calling her something else? There are a lot of people, Bill, that just go around taking the joy out of life. Well, anybody that calls me anything but "Marine" is going to hear from me. "Marine" is good enough for me. . . .

I can't sign myself as affectionately as I used to, Bill. You understand, I'm a soldier now and you wouldn't want me doing anything that wasn't in the Manual.

Yours till the cows come home,

—PVT. Martha L. Wilchinski, M.C.R.

PRIVATE WILCHINSKI FOUND THAT THE LIFE OF A LADY LEATHERNECK WAS LESS EXCITING THAN SHE HAD HOPED IT WOULD BE. IN A LATER LETTER TO BILL, SHE WROTE, "WHAT'LL I SAY TO MY GRANDCHILDREN, BILL? WHEN THEY ASK ME: 'WHAT DID YOU DO IN THE GREAT WAR, GRANDMA?' I'LL HAVE TO SAY: 'WASHING WINDOWS ON THE SECOND FLOOR.'"

Women marines were restricted to noncombat jobs. In addition to doing cleanup and clerical work, they worked at recruiting stations and Liberty bond rallies. Some were given the heartbreaking job of preparing letters to inform families that a loved one in the service had been killed. Violet Van Wagner, an eighteen-year-old recruit, recalled having to compose many such letters: "We would get the muster rolls, with the information about a man's death, and enter it onto record cards, with other details. The carnage was awful in those last months of the war, from the battles at Château Thierry, Belleau Wood, and the Meuse Argonne. . . . It was not a fun job."

Racism and Women Volunteers

Among the women eager to serve their country were 1,800 black nurses, fully trained and certified. Once again, however, racism stood in the way of skilled and eager volunteers. Nurses were desperately needed in France, but the U.S. Army Medical Department ignored these black women, even as it continued sending up calls for more volunteers. Army officials said that the problem was that they could not provide separate living quarters for them. During the entire course of the war, no black nurses were ever sent overseas.

When influenza spread throughout the United States in August 1918, the need for medical professionals became even more desperate, and some black nurses were sent to West Virginia. There they cared for coal miners and their families, who were essential to the war effort.

In addition to the doctors and nurses who tended to the soldiers' physical health, other volunteers were needed to ensure that servicemen remained mentally and emotionally fit. The YMCA in particular provided services to help keep up the soldiers' morale. "Canteens" were set up both on the homefront and

HELP HER CARRY ON!

"Miss America reports for service, Sir"

NATIONAL LEAGUE
for WOMAN'S SERVICE
The Woman Army
$200,000
needed for Vital War Work
SEPTEMBER 17 – 28

WOMEN VOLUNTEERS COULD TAKE PRIDE IN KNOWING THAT THEIR WORK WAS ESSENTIAL TO WINNING THE WAR.

behind the battle lines. At these informal social clubs, soldiers could relax, write letters home, enjoy a cup of coffee or hot chocolate, and generally recover from the horrors of the war. Nearly four thousand of the volunteers who ran these facilities in France were women, but again, because of racist attitudes, only nineteen were black.

Addie W. Hunton and Kathryn M. Johnson were among those nineteen. In their book, *Two Colored Women with the American*

Expeditionary Forces, they wrote about the acts of prejudice the African-American soldiers in France endured at the hands of their fellow countrymen. Signs on YMCA huts for servicemen proclaimed, "No Negroes Allowed," and white volunteers refused to serve blacks. "The fact that prejudice could follow us for three thousand miles across the Atlantic," said the women, "tremendously shocked us." The injustices African Americans endured "seared their souls like a hot iron, inflicted as they were at a time when these soldiers were rendering the American army and the nation a sacred service. . . . Always in those days there was fear of mutiny or rumors of mutiny. We felt most of the time that we were living close to the edge of a smoldering crater."

THE YMCA CANTEENS WERE A WELCOME SIGHT FOR SERVICEMEN AT HOME AND IN THE WAR ZONES.

THE ELEVENTH HOUR

The influenza has been raging all over the country with very high mortality, but here in W. [Washington, D.C.] the conditions were disgraceful. People died right and left from pure neglect, and bodies were lying about everywhere because there were no undertakers and no grave-diggers to dispose of them.

—AGNES ERNST MEYER,
WASHINGTON, D.C., FALL 1918

The Influenza Pandemic of 1918

In the late summer and fall of 1918, influenza (the flu) struck, and the disease proved even more deadly than the war. This was a pandemic—an epidemic affecting a wide geographic area—which spread like wildfire around the world. In the United States, a half million people died—ten times the number of Americans killed in the war. Worldwide, the disease claimed somewhere between 20 million and 100 million victims before disappearing the following spring. No one knows for sure exactly how many people died, because careful records were not kept everywhere. And the disease did spread everywhere. It reached every corner of the globe, sparing only a few remote islands and Australia. The influenza

PEOPLE WORE MASKS LIKE THIS ONE IN THE HOPE OF ESCAPING THE DEADLY FLU VIRUS.

pandemic killed more people more quickly than any other disease in the history of the world.

So many soldiers became sick that military campaigns were postponed and military camps in the United States were put under quarantine. Nearly 40 percent of the U.S. Navy came down with the disease, and the army estimated that more than one-third of its men were stricken. On the homefront, schools and other public buildings were closed and public gatherings were forbidden. So many Americans died in such a short time that the bodies had to be buried in mass graves.

In November 1918 W. H. Lefrancis, a relative of Joe Gaffney, who lived in Newark, New Jersey, described the impact of what he called the "worst scourge of a plague that the country ever experienced."

It has been awful, we had to establish emergency hospitals and call on the Red Cross and all the government equipment and forces in the City to lend their assistance in combatting the disease. The schools, Theatres, and Churches were closed and all assemblages of people were prohibited. In order to lessen the crowding of the trolley cars and railroad trains, the working hours were changed. In the cemeteries the dead were buried in trenches and even at that volunteer grave diggers had to be called for so that the corpses could be gotten underground.

And the great wonder is that there was not the slightest sign of a panic. Those who escaped the disease went along about their daily occupations just the same as ordinarily. Every day you would hear of some acquaintance who was stricken and in many cases in a day or two you would hear that he was dead. The normal response would be isn't it too bad. I think the war and the thought of what [the] boys over there are going through daily and the pluck and bravery [they] show in meeting the enemy, and besting him every where and every time has permeated all the folks at home so that they will face death and suffering with equal courage. . . .

In 1918 the cause of the influenza pandemic was a medical mystery. No one had ever seen a virus—the electron microscope had not yet been invented, and a virus is too small to be seen with an ordinary light microscope. But over the years evidence gathered from victims of the disaster has provided scientists with some clues. Tissue samples taken from bodies of flu victims in 1918 were stored in hospital basements and military archives, and some researchers have recently analyzed these. Other researchers have searched for bodies that were preserved well enough to still contain the virus. In 1997 scientists dug up a mass grave in the permafrost, or permanently frozen ground, of a village in Alaska. One of the bodies provided samples of tissue with the virus still intact. Using these samples, the scientists were able to identify the virus; they are still trying to learn what made it so deadly.

"All Over But the Shouting"

At the eleventh hour on the eleventh day of the eleventh month of 1918, the World War ended. Bells pealed from churches all over the United States, and people poured out into the streets to celebrate the armistice. U.S. troops had helped turn the tide and defeat the Germans.

IN NEW YORK CITY, NEWS THAT THE WAR HAD ENDED BROUGHT THRONGS OF PEOPLE INTO THE STREETS TO CELEBRATE.

I N A LETTER TO HIS COUSIN JOE GAFFNEY, W. H. LEFRANCIS DESCRIBED AMERICANS' JOYOUS REACTION TO NEWS OF THE WAR'S END.

Newark N. J. Nov 11th 1918

Dear Cousin Joe—

Your very welcome letter to Bessie has just come to hand, and, as Miss Bessie is downtown taking part in the joyous celebration I can't wait for her to come home so I have transgressed all proprieties and opened and read your letter. . . .

We have feared for you ever since you went over and have scanned the New York Times every day fearing that your name might appear in the lists, but your letter removes all doubts up to the date given, and from today forward it is all over but the shouting. . . .

Joe, I am very sorry for you and all the rest of the boys who are over there today. . . . . .ays that this country or any other country has ever s . . . . .ir victories and the crushing of Germany, the abdic . . . . .r and the Crown Prince. Everything goes, the louder . . . . more fun you are having. Parades are to be counte . . . .'t get a brass band, why a dozen tin wash tubs will be . . . . regards work, nothing doing today. This is no comm . . . . .ave gone clean crazy. If you have not got food in the . . . . .e from the neighbors. The stores are all closed . . . . they will close about noon time because they w . . . .

. . . . .n any more than I can describe it. It started at 4 o' . . . . .ing of every factory whistle, the ringing of all the . . . . .ne through the street long before daylight, with a . . . . , sounding the reveille, and then played the Star Spangled Banner, everybody knew what was meant. For we had a previous celebration on last Thursday on a premature report that Germany had surrendered, and that the war was over. But everyone will tell you that all this is merely a preliminary training for the day when our boys come home. . . .

I understand that you boys are always pleased to receive letters from the folks at home and for that reason I am writing you leaving it to Bessie to write for herself, and I think the best time to write is at once, so accordingly I have practiced what I preach and hope this will find you in good health and spirits and that if I don't see you before long we may have the pleasure of hearing from you.

Yours very truly,
W. H. Lefrancis
130 S. 9th St.

Le Petit Journal

ADMINISTRATION
61, RUE LAFAYETTE, 61
Les manuscrits ne sont pas rendus
On s'abonne sans frais
dans tous les bureaux de poste

15 CENT.
29me Année

SUPPLÉMENT ILLUSTRÉ

15 CENT.

ABONNEMENTS

Numéro 1.483

DIMANCHE 25 MAI 1919

France et Colonies....   SIX MOIS UN AN
                          5 fr.   8 fr.
Étranger ....   9 fr.   10 fr.

LA SÉANCE HISTORIQUE DE VERSAILLES
Remise aux plénipotentiaires allemands des conditions de paix des Alliés

AT THE PEACE TALKS IN VERSAILLES, A CITY OUTSIDE PARIS, THE ALLIES PRESENT THEIR
TERMS TO THE GERMAN DELEGATION.

Soon President Wilson was on his way to Paris to participate
in the peace talks. Months earlier, the president had proposed a
peace program called the Fourteen Points, which called for a just
and unselfish peace. He believed that humiliating the defeated

nations would only ensure another war. The French and British, however, thought otherwise, and their wishes won out in the peace settlement. The Versailles Treaty of 1919 heaped crushing economic burdens on the Germans.

As President Wilson had feared, the terms of the peace did indeed sow the seeds for another war. Adolf Hitler, a soldier in the Great War, would rise to power, calling on Germans to avenge their nation's two million war dead and to reclaim their place in the world. In little more than twenty years after the Great War was over, Europe would again be in flames. That conflagration would engulf the world in the bloody conflict known as World War II.

CONCLUSION: AFTER THE ARMISTICE

Poet Langston Hughes described what the end of World War I meant for African Americans:

That November the First World War ended. In Cleveland, everybody poured into the streets to celebrate the Armistice. Negroes, too, although Negroes were increasingly beginning to wonder where, for them, was that democracy they had fought to preserve. In Cleveland, a liberal city, the color line began to be drawn tighter and tighter. Theaters and restaurants in the downtown area began to refuse to accommodate colored people. Landlords doubled and tripled the rents at the approach of a dark tenant. And when the white soldiers came back from the war, Negroes were often discharged from their jobs and white men hired in their places.

LANGSTON HUGHES, IN A PORTRAIT PAINTED ABOUT 1925

Most Americans who had fought in Europe were back home by the spring of 1919. That summer exploded in a series of race riots, one of the worst of which took place in Chicago, where thirty-eight people died. Serious riots also shook towns in Texas, Tennessee, and Nebraska, and even hit the nation's capital. In the last six months of the year, seventy-six blacks were lynched.

The situation appeared so dismal that some African Americans despaired of ever finding dignity in the United States. It would be many decades before race relations would improve.

• • •

From late 1918 through the middle of 1920, the United States was rocked by strikes—3,600 in all, including the first nationwide steel strike, a citywide general strike in Seattle, and a police strike in Boston. Further heightening tensions, terrorists sent bombs to U.S. Attorney General A. Mitchell Palmer and other government officials. The strikes and acts of terrorism gave rise to the "Red scare," a fear that radicals were plotting a communist revolution.

Attorney General Palmer responded by launching raids that targeted "dangerous aliens": radicals, immigrants, nonwhites, and union members. Nearly 250 men and women were arrested and deported to Russia on December 21, 1919, some without a chance

SOLDIERS IN BOSTON ROUND UP STRIKING POLICEMEN IN 1919.

to say goodbye to their families. In January 1920 "Palmer raids" netted another 4,000 people.

Fear of foreigners was fired by articles in American popular magazines arguing that the Nordic races—northern Europeans—were superior to other peoples, and that immigrants from southern and eastern Europe were a menace to society. Laws were passed in 1921 and 1924 that severely limited immigration, discriminating particularly against southern and eastern Europeans. These laws joined legislation from the early 1900s that had sharply limited immigration from Asian countries. In signing the 1924 law, President Calvin Coolidge said, "America must be kept American." In this atmosphere of distrust and intolerance, the

IN BOSTON IN 1920, SUSPECTED "REDS" ARE CHAINED TOGETHER, WAITING TO BE TAKEN TO THE EMIGRATION STATION, WHERE THEY WILL BE QUESTIONED AND POSSIBLY DEPORTED.

postwar years saw a resurgence of the Ku Klux Klan, whose members intimidated and terrorized foreigners, Jews, Catholics, and African Americans.

• • •

For women, the end of war brought signs of progress. For years women's groups had been active supporters of movements to control or ban the consumption of alcohol. In early 1919 the Eighteenth Amendment to the Constitution introduced Prohibition—laws outlawing the production and sale of liquor. Prohibition was regarded as a victory for women. Almost immediately, however, a movement began to repeal the amendment.

A more lasting victory was the passage of the Nineteenth Amendment in 1920, giving women the right to vote. African-American women, though, would have to wait decades—until the civil rights movement of the 1950s and 1960s—before they could fully exercise that right.

• • •

The United States emerged from World War I a different country. The lives of hundreds of thousands of men and women had been changed forever. Americans had experienced horrors they would never forget, they had suffered wounds that would not heal, they had lost loved ones. Many who had never been away from home before had traveled to another continent and seen other cultures up close.

More than half the population of the U.S. now lived in cities, and the number of African Americans in northern cities had greatly increased. Immigration was a trickle of what it had been. Women were envisioning new possibilities in work and in politics, although it would be decades before many of these dreams were realized. For African Americans, the struggle for equality was just beginning.

TIME LINE OF WORLD WAR I EVENTS

1914

June 28
Archduke Franz Ferdinand is assassinated in Bosnia by a Serb.

July 28
Austria-Hungary declares war on Serbia.

August 1
Germany declares war on Russia.

August 3
Germany declares war on France.

August 4
German army invades Belgium.

August 5
Austria-Hungary declares war on Russia. Great Britain, France, and Russia declare war on Germany.

August 12–13
Great Britain and France declare war on Austria-Hungary.

September 15
First trenches are dug along the Western Front, eventually stretching 475 miles, through Belgium and France from the North Sea to the Swiss border.

October 31
Turkish empire joins the Central Powers.

1915

January 19
German zeppelins begin bombing British towns and cities from the air—the first time aircraft are used against civilians.

April 22
Germans launch the first attack of poisonous gas, against French-Algerian troops in Belgium.

April 25
The Allies land along the Turkish coast on the Gallipoli Peninsula, seeking to re-open the Turkish blockade of the Dardanelles, the only sea route to southern Russia.

May 7
Off the coast of Ireland, a German submarine torpedoes the British passenger liner *Lusitania*.

May 23
Italy enters the war on the side of the Allies.

1916

February 21
Germans attack the French city of Verdun. Battle continues for ten months.

May 31
Battle of Jutland in the North Sea, one of the largest sea battles ever. Both sides claim victory and thousands of lives are lost. The German fleet will not leave the harbor for the rest of the war.

July 1
The British, with French help, begin a large-scale attack along the Somme River in northwest France.

September 15
The British make a new assault in the battle of the Somme, using a new weapon, the tank.

November 7
Woodrow Wilson is elected U.S. president for a second term.

November 18
Battle of the Somme ends with 650,000 German, 420,000 British, and 195,000 French casualties.

December 18
The French retake most of the territory around Verdun.

1917

February 1
German submarines begin unrestricted warfare in British waters.

February 3
The U.S. breaks relations with Germany.

March 15
U.S. merchant ships are torpedoed by German subs. Three are sunk.
Russian government overthrown; Czar Nicholas II abdicates as provisional government is installed.

April 6
The U.S. declares war on Germany.

May 18
The Selective Service Act becomes law.

June 24
The first U.S. troops reach France.

October 24–November 12
Germans rout Italians at Battle of Caporetto; 400,000 Italian soldiers desert and go home.

November 7
Bolshevik Socialists, led by Lenin, take over Russian government.

December 15
Russia signs armistice with Germany; fighting on Eastern Front ends.

1918

January 8
President Wilson announces his Fourteen-Point plan for peace.

March 3
Russia signs treaty of Brest-Litovsk and leaves the war.

March 11
Influenza breaks out at an army camp in Kansas, the first outbreak in the U.S. By fall the disease will have become a pandemic.

March 21
The Germans launch first of five major offensives on the Western Front and push back the Allies.

May 28
The Americans launch attack at Cantigny, northwest of the Marne River in France, and win a major battle against the Germans.

June 4
German offensive halted. Battle between U.S. and German troops at Château-Thierry in France ends in a U.S. victory.

June 25
American offensive recaptures Belleau Wood, west of Château-Thierry, as German positions fall to the Allies.

July 15
Second battle of the Marne. By July 21, Germans are in full retreat.

August 8
The British, Canadians, and Australians launch an attack at Amiens, using tanks to push back the Germans.

August 30
General Pershing takes command of U.S. troops at Saint-Mihiel, occupied by Germans since the beginning of the war.

September 12
American infantry breaks through German lines on first day of Saint-Mihiel offensive, defeating the enemy in four days.

September 26
The Meuse-Argonne offensive begins, to push the Germans out of France.

September 29
The Allies break through the Hindenburg Line.

October 4
The Germans dispatch cable to President Wilson, asking for peace.

October 12
Germany accepts Fourteen Points as condition of peace.

October 30
Turkish Empire surrenders to the Allies.

November 3
Austria-Hungary surrenders to the Allies.

November 9
Kaiser Wilhelm II of Germany abdicates and flees to the Netherlands.

November 11
The Armistice is signed and fighting ends on the Western Front. The war is over.

GLOSSARY

alien A person living in a country who is not a citizen of that country.

anarchist A person who believes that government oppresses people and that therefore all forms of government should be abolished.

armistice An agreement to stop fighting; a truce.

conscientious objector Someone who refuses to serve in the military because of moral or religious reasons.

conscription Compulsory enrollment in the armed forces; draft.

espionage The act of spying, usually to gain information about government activities and plans.

Jim Crow laws Laws dating from the 1880s that allowed separate schools, movie houses, drinking fountains, seating on trains and buses, etc., for blacks and whites in the United States. The laws were based on the argument that such facilities could be "separate but equal," although, in fact, they discriminated against African Americans. It was not until 1954 that these laws were ruled unconstitutional by the Supreme Court, which found that separate was by definition unequal.

migrant A person who moves, or migrates, from one place to another.

pacifist Someone who opposes war or violence as a means of resolving conflict.

propaganda Information and ideas spread to convince people to take a particular point of view.

radical Favoring extreme changes in political and social systems and institutions.

ration To distribute items—usually food, but also fuel, clothing, and other goods—in predetermined amounts in order to conserve them and distribute them fairly.

sedition The encouragement of rebellion against the government.

segregation Separation of people according to race.

TO FIND OUT MORE

Nonfiction

Dolan, Edward F. *America in World War I*. Brookfield, CT: Millbrook Press, 1996.
Clearly presented, easy to read, with lots of illustrations, time lines, maps, and charts. A good overview of the war.

Foreman, Michael. *War Game*. New York: Arcade Publishing, 1994.
A picture book that tells the true story of Christmas Eve 1914, when British and German troops climbed out of their trenches and played a game of soccer together.

Fradin, Dennis Brindell, and Judith Bloom Fradin. *Ida B. Wells: Mother of the Civil Rights Movement*. New York: Clarion, 2000.
A biography of the journalist who used her writing to fight Jim Crow laws and, most especially, lynching. The book draws upon Wells's autobiography, her diaries, and letters and editorials she wrote, giving a sense of the person as well as her historical importance. Includes archival photos.

Gay, Kathlyn, and Martin Gay. *World War I*. New York: Twenty-First Century Books, 1995.
A title in the Voices from the Past series, including many first-person accounts, some from interviews with World War I veterans, some from written sources.

Hamilton, Virginia. *W. E. B. Du Bois: A Biography*. New York: Thomas Y. Crowell, 1972.
The story of the Harvard-educated scholar and activist who was one of the founders of the NAACP and an ardent civil rights activist before, during, and after the Great War. By the distinguished children's book author.

Hoobler, Dorothy, and Thomas Hoobler. *An Album of World War I*. New York: Franklin Watts, 1976.
Packed with black-and-white photos, this book provides an eyewitness account of the war, with emphasis on Europe. Includes maps showing how the world changed with the war.

———. *The Trenches: Fighting on the Western Front in World War I*. New York: G. P. Putnam's Sons, 1978.
Describes the combat experiences of English, French, and German soldiers during the war.

Katz, William Loren. *Minorities in American History.* Vol. 4, *From the Progressive Era to the Great Depression, 1900–1929.* New York: Franklin Watts, 1974.
An account of how African Americans, Hispanics, Jews, Native Americans, and other minorities fared in the first part of the twentieth century in the U.S.

McGowen, Tom. *World War I.* New York: Franklin Watts, 1993.
A year-by-year account of the battles and political changes that took place from 1914 to 1918.

Meltzer, Milton. *Ain't Gonna Study War No More: The Story of America's Peace Seekers.* New York: HarperCollins, 1985.
A history of the many ways in which Americans have protested wars, refused the draft, and argued against militarism, from colonial times through the calls for nuclear disarmament in the 1980s.

———. *The Black Americans: A History in Their Own Words, 1619–1983.* New York: HarperTrophy, 1984.
A collection that draws on a wide range of African-American voices, from ordinary people to famous writers, politicians, and other spokespeople. A vivid, moving history.

Rees, Rosemary. *The Western Front.* Crystal Lake, IL: Rigby Interactive Library, 1997.
A title in the History through Sources series, this book intersperses quotes from people who lived the war—officers, volunteers, ordinary soldiers—with text explaining the war and suggesting areas for discussion.

Stein, Judith E. *I Tell My Heart: The Art of Horace Pippin.* Philadelphia: Pennsylvania Academy of the Fine Arts, 1993.
Articles about aspects of the art of Horace Pippin, an African American who served in the 369th Infantry Regiment in France. Although he was wounded and suffered permanent disability of his right arm, he went on to become a highly regarded painter. Some of his paintings depict war scenes and some represent themes of the struggle for racial justice.

Waldstreicher, David. *Emma Goldman.* New York: Chelsea House, 1990.
A title in the American Women of Achievement series, a biography of the political activist who was imprisoned and deported for taking up such causes as anarchism, birth control, women's rights, and opposing the draft. Illustrated with historical photos. Introduction by Matina Horner, president of Radcliffe College.

Fiction

Cather, Willa. *One of Ours*. New York: Vintage Books, 1991.
A novel about a Nebraska farm boy who is killed fighting on the Western Front. The book won the Pulitzer Prize in 1923.

Corcoran, Barbara. *The Private War of Lillian Adams*. New York: Atheneum, 1989.
When Lil's favorite cousin leaves for Europe to fight in the Great War, Lil starts looking for spies everywhere in her hometown of Brookline, Massachusetts. Richly evocative of life on the homefront during the war.

Hemingway, Ernest. *A Farewell to Arms*. New York: Chelsea House, 2000.
One of the classic novels of the Great War, written for adults but with a style and story that are readable and interesting for younger readers, too. Hemingway, who was a young man during the war, volunteered to drive an ambulance in Italy before the U.S. entered the war.

Remarque, Erich Maria. *All Quiet on the Western Front*. New York: Ballantine Books, 1982.
Another classic novel of the war, this one written by a veteran of the German army who was sixteen when the war broke out. The novel is a powerful statement against wars and the hatred that causes them.

Rostkowski, Margaret I. *After the Dancing Days*. New York: Harper & Row, 1986.
The story of a Midwestern family after the war, when the veterans come home, many permanently disabled and all changed forever.

On the Internet*

"My History Is America's History: A Millennium Project of the National Endowment for the Humanities," at
http://www.myhistory.org
A gathering place for sharing family stories, which includes a guidebook for making your own contributions, sites for posting your family's favorite stories, and links to other websites.

"Wartime Letters of Kansas City's James E. (Ned) Henschel" at
http:www.umkc.edu/KCAA/DUSTYSHELF/DS17-3.HTM
Includes photos and narrative.

Websites change from time to time. For additional on-line information, check with the media specialist at your local library.

BIBLIOGRAPHY

Aptheker, Herbert, ed. *A Documentary History of the Negro People in the United States: From the Emergence of the N.A.A.C.P. to the Beginning of the New Deal, 1910–1932*. Secaucus, NJ: Citadel Press, 1973.

Coben, Stanley. "A Study in Nativism: The American Red Scare of 1919–1920." In *The Causes and Consequences of World War I*, edited by John Milton Cooper, Jr. New York: Quadrangle Books, 1972.

Commager, Henry Steele, ed. *Documents of American History*. New York: Appleton-Century-Crofts, Inc., 1949.

Commager, Henry Steele, and Allan Nevins, eds. *The Heritage of America*. Boston: Little, Brown, 1949.

Cooper, John Milton, Jr. *Pivotal Decades: The United States, 1900–1920*. New York: W. W. Norton, 1990.

Cowing, Kemper Frey, ed. *"Dear Folks at Home": The Glorious Story of the United States Marines in France As Told by Their Letters from the Battlefield*. Boston: Houghton Mifflin, 1919.

Ellis, Edward Robb. *Echoes of Distant Thunder: Life in the United States, 1914–1918*. New York: Kodansha International, 1996.

Falk, Candace Serena. *Love, Anarchy, and Emma Goldman*. New Brunswick, NJ: Rutgers University Press, 1990.

Farwell, Byron. *Over There: The United States in the Great War, 1917–1918*. New York: W. W. Norton, 1999.

Ferrell, Robert H. *Woodrow Wilson and World War I, 1917–1921*. New York: Harper & Row, 1985.

Fishel, Leslie H., Jr., and Benjamin Quarles. *The Black American: A Documentary History*. New York: William Morrow, 1970.

Gavin, Lettie. *American Women in World War I: They Also Served*. Niwot, CO: University Press of Colorado, 1997.

Graham, Katharine. *Personal History*. New York: Vintage Books, 1998.

Harries, Meirion, and Susie Harries. *The Last Days of Innocence: America at War, 1917–1918*. New York: Random House, 1997.

Henri, Florette. *Black Migration: Movement North, 1900–1920*. New York: Anchor Books, 1976.

Hughes, Langston. *The Big Sea*. New York: Hill and Wang, 1998.

Keegan, John. *The First World War*. New York: Alfred A. Knopf, 1998.

Kennedy, David M. *Over Here: The First World War and American Society*. Oxford: Oxford University Press, 1980.

Kolata, Gina. *Flu: The Story of the Great Influenza Pandemic of 1918 and the Search for the Virus That Caused It*. New York: Farrar, Straus & Giroux, 1999.

Ladd-Taylor, Molly. *Raising a Baby the Government Way: Mothers' Letters to the Children's Bureau, 1915–1932*. New Brunswick, NJ: Rutgers University Press, 1986.

Lerner, Gerda, ed. *Black Women in White America: A Documentary History*. New York: Vintage Books, 1992.

McGovern, James R. "The American Woman's Pre-World War I Freedom in Manners and Morals." In *The Causes and Consequences of World War I*, edited by John Milton Cooper, Jr. New York: Quadrangle Books, 1972.

Muncy, Robyn. *Creating a Female Dominion in American Reform, 1890–1935*. Oxford: Oxford University Press, 1991.

Murphy, Paul L. *World War I and the Origin of Civil Liberties in the United States*. New York: W. W. Norton, 1979.

Sangster, Ellen Geer. *"A Grain of Mustard Seed": Memories of Eight Decades*. Amherst, MA: Green Knight Press, 1978.

Schaffer, Ronald. *America in the Great War: The Rise of the War Welfare State*. New York: Oxford University Press, 1991.

Scott, Emmett J., ed. "Letters of Negro Migrants of 1916–1918." *Journal of Negro History*. No. 4, no. 3 (July 1919) and no. 4 (October 1919).

Vaughn, Stephen L. *Holding Fast the Inner Lines: Democracy, Nationalism, and the Committee on Public Information*. Chapel Hill: University of North Carolina Press, 1980.

Ward, Geoffrey C., and Ken Burns. *Baseball: An Illustrated History*. New York: Alfred A. Knopf, 1994.

Winter, J. M. *The Experience of World War I*. New York: Oxford University Press, 1995.

NOTES ON QUOTES

The quotations in this book are from the following sources:

Introduction: The Great War
p. 10 "The European nations" James and Wells, *America and the Great War*, p. 2.
p. 10 "We have never appreciated so keenly" ibid., p. 3.

Chapter One: Making the World Safe for Democracy
p. 12 "Over there, over there" Farwell, *Over There*, p. 36.
p. 12 "We will not choose" Commager and Nevins, *Heritage of America*, p. 1071.
p. 13 "The United States must be neutral," Woodrow Wilson's message to the Senate, *Documents of American History*, p. 276.
p. 14 "Of course, like most of my contemporaries" Sangster, *"A Grain of Mustard Seed,"* p. 32.
p. 17 "The military tent" Kennedy, *Over Here*, p. 17.
p. 20 "It is not an army" Vaughn, *Holding Fast the Inner Lines*, p. 4.
p. 21 "big, ringing statements" Vaughn, Holding Fast the Inner Lines, p. 17.
p. 24 "to keep the German soldiers" Kennedy, *Over Here*, p. 55.
p. 24 "you won't get your steel" Cooper, *Pivotal Decades*, p. 289.
p. 24 "We were woefully ignorant" Farwell, *Over There*, pp. 94–95.
p. 26 "Guess you have heard" Gaffney-Ahearn Correspondence, New York Public Library, January 17, 1918.
p. 26 "You should see" ibid., January 28, 1918.
p. 26 "all the saloons" ibid., January 22, 1918.
p. 26 "I suppose the camp clocks" ibid., March 24, 1918.
p. 27 "mobilize the spirit" Kennedy, *Over Here*, p. 118.
p. 28 "Blood or Bread" James and Wells, *America and the Great War*, pp. 63–64.
p. 28 "Be patriotic" Dolan, *America in World War I*, p. 38.
p. 28 "serve the cause of freedom" James and Wells, *America and the Great War*, p. 63.
p. 31 "Beat Back the Hun" Vaughn, *Holding Fast the Inner Lines*, p. 163.
p. 31 "Lick a Stamp" James and Wells, *America and the Great War*, p. 65.

Chapter Two: Intolerance
p. 34 "Once lead this people" Harries and Harries, *Last Days of Innocence*, p. 293.
p. 35 "Congress shall make" U.S. Constitution, amend. 1.
p. 36 "uttering, printing, writing" Cooper, *Pivotal Decades*, p. 298.
p. 36 "We, who came from Europe" Falk, *Love, Anarchy, and Emma Goldman*, p. 156.
p. 36 "the most dangerous woman" ibid.
p. 39 "cries for peace" Vaughn, *Holding Fast the Inner Lines*, p. 231.
p. 40 [Baseball sidebar] "players in the draft age" Ward and Burns, *Baseball*, p. 131.
p. 40 [Baseball sidebar] "As the crowd of 19,274 spectators" ibid., p. 132.
p. 42 "The master class has always declared wars" Meltzer, *Ain't Gonna Study War No More*, p. 157.
p. 44 "Well, I guess nobody can say" Harries and Harries, *Last Days of Innocence*, p. 296.

Chapter Three: African Americans and the Great War

p. 46 "If this is our country" Keegan, *The First World War*, p. 374.

p. 50 "Our young men are so anxious to serve" J. Milton Waldron to Woodrow Wilson, May 11, 1917, Woodrow Wilson Papers, Series 4, file 152, Library of Congress.

p. 55 "I talked with all classes of colored people" W. T. B. Williams, "The Negro Exodus from the South," in U.S. Department of Labor, Division of Negro Economics, Negro Migration in 1916–1917, reprinted in Fishel and Quarles, *The Black American*, p. 394 ff.

Chapter Four: Women's Work

p. 61 "[The rain was] cold and continuous" Gavin, *American Women in World War I*, p. 58.

p. 61 "the type of girl" McGovern, "American Woman's Pre-World War I Freedom," p. 275.

p. 64 "Saving babies is a vital part" and "a year in which" Muncy, *Creating a Female Dominion*, pp. 97, 98.

p. 64 "If we decide that the abolition of poverty" ibid, p. 98.

p. 65 "Went to a suffragist meeting" *Fishawack Papers*, Vol. III, p. 265.

p. 67 "Enroll women in the naval service" Gavin, *American Women in World War I*, p. 2.

p. 68 "I never did like this 'ette' business" ibid., p. 4.

p. 68 "intelligent young women" ibid., p. 26.

p. 69 "What'll I say" Cowing, *"Dear Folks at Home,"* p. 21.

p. 70 "We would get the muster roles" ibid., pp. 33–34.

p. 72 "The fact that prejudice could follow us" Hunton and Johnson, *Two Colored Women*, p. 138.

p. 72 "seared their souls like a hot iron" ibid., p. 235.

Chapter Five: The Eleventh Hour

p. 73 "The influenza has been raging" Graham, *Personal History*, p. 29.

p. 74 "the worst scourge" Gaffney-Ahearn Correspondence, New York Public Library, November 11, 1918.

p. 75 "It has been awful" ibid.

Conclusion: After the Armistice

p. 80 "That November" Hughes, *The Big Sea*, p. 51.

p. 82 "America must be kept American" Katz, *Minorities in American History*, p. 71.

INDEX

Page numbers for illustrations are in **boldface**

ABOUT THE AUTHOR

PHOTOGRAPH BY ALEXANDER GEORGE

"What I love about history is the small stories, the stories of ordinary people. People who lived through World War I—my grandparents and your great-grandparents—helped write the history of the war, just as much as the presidents and the generals did. It was exciting to get to know some of these people, to hold their letters, to see their handwriting, to read their words.

"I was eager to write this book because I have been interested in World War I for a long time, but for a reason that had little to do with United States history. That war was a turning point in the history of the Middle East, one of my favorite parts of the world. The war changed the Middle East forever. I was fascinated to learn the ways in which the war also changed the United States."

Linda S. George has taught Middle East history and literature at Columbia University in New York and at Drew University in Madison, New Jersey. She has a Ph.D. from Harvard University in linguistics and has studied and worked in many parts of the Middle East. This is her second book for Marshall Cavendish.

Ms. George lives in New Jersey with her husband, Richard, and their son, Alexander.